OVER COMING TIMIDITY AND COWARDICE

EVERY MAN'S TERRORIST

By Joyce J. Toney

XULON PRESS

DEDICATION

⤳

To my wonderful mother, Gracie, who on November 26, 1996 went home to be with her Lord and Savior Jesus Christ.

To my daughter, Jerica, who always encourages me to look beyond human impossibilities to the *extraordinary* possibilities of God.

ACKNOWLEDGEMENTS

I am eternally grateful for the manifested love of the Father, Son, and Holy Spirit, which enfolds me. El Shaddai's love for me encourages me to always press forward-forward-forward. I give God honor and praise for ALL He has done for me and through me, for without Him, I am nothing.

I want to thank my husband, Guenther, without whose continuing encouragement and support I could not have completed this work.

In addition, my daughter Jerica and family, especially Ruthie, Linda, and Robert, their faith in me was and is an invaluable empowerment.

EL SHADDAI, MY HEAVENLY FATHER,

You know every thing about me. You know my every weakness, my inadequacies, and my fears. Hear me and know my thoughts, cleanse me, and deliver me, from all my fears.

Strengthen me where I am weak and empower me by Your Holy Spirit to overcome these inadequacies that I may be totally independent of them and dependent on You.

Give me the desire to appropriate Your courage. Father I thank you for continuous victory over timidity and cowardice.

Jehovah, You are my hope and my praise.
You are my Victory!

TABLE OF CONTENTS

"For God did not give us a spirit of timidity (of cowardice, of craven and cringing and fawning fear), but (He has given us a spirit) of power and of love and of calm and well-balanced mind and discipline and self-control"
(2 Timothy 1:7)

INTRODUCTION

The Lord shook me one day while I was crying out to Him to deliver me from depression and constant fatigue. I was plagued with depression and fatigue for over two years. I work an eight-hour job, which is very stressful, and I pastor a small fellowship.

I was so depressed at times that I felt as if I carried a dark cloud around me. It was as if I carried an umbrella over me constantly raining down darkness. I felt as if I had my own special set of weighty shackles with iron balls on my ankles.

Then the voice of the Lord came to me and said, "Fast". I thought, *fast... I hardly have energy to go to work. I sleep from 6 P.M. until 4:30 A.M. and you want me to fast?*

Unenthusiastically, I obeyed God. I had been on the fast for about two days when the Lord spoke to me and said "coward". I said, "Coward? Lord, what does *coward* have to do with this depression?" On the fourth day of the fast the Lord spoke to me again and said, "No coward will enter into my kingdom."

My mind just stopped and I was shaken in my spirit. I asked God, "What does that have to do with me?" He replied, "Your problem is that you are allowing the spirit of timidity and the spirit cowardice to rule your life. These spirits are slowly sifting the life out of you and eventually will cause you to turn away from me. That turning away will lead you to the second death." I asked the Lord to help me. He told me, "I have already given you authority over these spirits."

Yes, I repented, confessed my sin of disobedience and unbelief. I was disobedient to the authority that God had given me. I had failed to walk in the authority Jesus conferred on me.

I had allowed despondency and depression to come into my life by way of the spirit of timidity and the spirit of cowardice. This, in God's eyes was unbelief. I had failed to have confidence in Him to deliver me. I had surrendered. I asked God to forgive me. I heard the Lord say, "The blood." I immediately started pleading the blood of Jesus over me. I rebuked the spirit of timidity and the spirit of cowardice and a tremendous heaviness lifted from me.

The next day I noticed that I had an energy that I had not experienced in over two years. I stayed awake until 11 P.M. whereas I normally fell asleep around 6 P.M. For me, this was a miracle! The depression and fatigue was completely gone. Agitation and touchiness was also gone. Short temperedness and the angry feelings that had pledged me for years were gone too. I was and I still am a new person.

The spirit of timidity and the spirit of cowardice is the theme of this book. God has delivered me from these subtle and dangerous enemies. God has brought them from the shadows and shined His light of truth on them and exposed them.

I am aware that the enemy only leaves us alone for a season, if then. However, I know with all certainty that Jesus Christ is the Victor and I am in Him, therefore I stand in victory.

Through God's amazing love, He has enlightened me regarding these vicious enemies and how to wage war against them. It is my prayer that God will provide me the grace to teach others what He has taught me.

In Jesus' Love & In His Army,

Joyce J. Toney

CHAPTER ONE

COWARDS WILL NOT ENTER HEAVEN

⥈

"But as for the cowards and the ignoble and the contemptible and the cravenly lacking in courage and the cowardly submissive, and as for the unbelieving and faithless, and as for the depraved and defiled with abominations, and as for murderers and the lewd and adulterous and the practicers of magic arts and the idolaters (those who give supreme devotion to anyone or anything other than God) and all liars (those who knowingly convey untruth by word or deed)—(all of these shall have) their part in the lake that blazes with fire and brimstone. This is the second death."(Revelation 21:8)

God has decreed that no cowards, nor any form of cowardice will enter heaven. As a result of this decree, we would think that there would be no cowards or any of its forms in the Body of Christ. Sadly, this is not the case. Volumes of books have been published on fear and overcoming fear, yet I have not read a single one that deals with the consequences that God has mandated for those that are the timid, the fearful, and the cowardly.

There is a real consequent in failing to deal with the unseen forces that keep people bound by timidity and cowardice. Although we can ignore certain sections in the Bible because it does not fit our comfort zone, ignoring it will not remove the consequences of the disobedience to it.

God's standards as His laws are eternal. Neither will be altered because of our comfort zone. There is a future judgment for everyone. Hebrews chapter nine and verse twenty-seven states, *"And just as it is **appointed** for (all) men once to die, and after that the (certain) judgment."*

Thus we all should want to know, by what standards God will judge us. What category of people will and what category will not be judged? Part of Jesus' Gospel is who will and who will not. I believe that we have gotten to far away from the "who will not". We are out of balance so to speak. Some of the present day churches (assemblies) have lowered their standards but God has not lowered His.

Unlike our modern churches, the *criterion* for entrance and membership in the early church were quite different. In the majority of churches today there is no new convert initiation or preparation for service. I'm not speaking of the new member's class where the statement of faith of the church is discussed and the new convert is given a six-week training program on all of his or her rights as a new Christian.

On the contrary, I am speaking of the *discipleship* and *proving* of the new convert. For example, the initiation process established by the early Church encompassed a period of deliverance for all new converts.

According to the Hippolytus' *"Apostolic Tradition"* written in the early part of the third century, it was mandatory for the candidates for baptism to undergo exorcisms, which were scheduled daily during the period of initiation, instructions, and preparation, process of the new convert.

The instruction and preparation was from twenty-four to thirty-six months depending on the growth and spiritual development of the convert and candidates for membership in to the body of believers. These converts had to pass through a three or four stage instruction and preparation process for baptism.

Baptism was not just a dip in the water, as in some of our modern churches; it was considered the spiritual counterpart to circumcision as stipulated in the Old Testament. It initiated the proselyte into the company of believers. It was the symbol of the New Covenant, identifying the person as one of God's people.

In addition, its concept was to convey the gift of the Holy Spirit, which would illuminate and enable the believer for spiritual combat. It was also symbolic to the believer's identification with the death, burial, and resurrection of Jesus Christ. The new convert had to not only accept Jesus Christ as Lord and Savior but the believer had to renounce Satan and all of his works as a part of his instructional and preoperational process for baptism.

They were anointed with special exorcised oil as part of the preparation process in a final ceremony of exorcism to banish all evil spirits before entering the water. For further reading in this area, study the "Teaching of the Apostles" and "Apostolic Tradition". (See appendix for further information.)

Moreover, I believe that spirits such as timidity and cowardice would not plague the church if some of the traditions of the "Apostolic Tradition" were still a part of the new convert initiation and preparation for membership into the Body of Christ.

With that said we must aim at and meet all the conditions God has set for entrance into His presence and His Kingdom. In John chapter ten, Jesus said:

"I ASSURE you, most solemnly I tell you, he who does not enter by the door into the sheepfold, but climbs up some other way (elsewhere, from some other quarter) is a thief and a robber."

(John 10:1)

All our efforts and standards to enter in the Kingdom of God must go through the holy sifter of Jesus, who has already set the standards and conditions to enter His kingdom.

In Revelation 21:8, as shown above, Jesus provides John the Apostle, a list of those who *will not* enter the Kingdom of God. I believe that this list is worth noting:

- The Cowards
- The Ignoble
- The Contemptible
- The Cravenly lacking in courage
- The Cowardly submissive
- The Unbelieving
- The Faithless
- The Deprave
- The Defiled with abominations
- The Lewd
- The Adulterous
- The Practitioner's of magic arts
- The Idolaters (Those who give supreme devotion to anyone or anything other than God)
- The Lairs (Those who knowingly convey untruth by word or deed)

Jesus clearly articulates that people who fall into either one of these categories will, "Have their part in the lake that blazes with fire and brimstone. This is the second death."(Rev 21:8) Many of us think that we are on fire for God, but in all actuality, we have the sparks from hell lighting the torch of our personality and our Christian walk.

Before I go on, I want to state that there is a distinct difference between Christians who live by the standards of the world standards and Christians who live by Biblical standards. God gave the Law of Holiness and Judgment to Moses. (See the Five Books of Moses, in general and Leviticus chapter 20 in particular). I am not including the Temple rituals here, although they do point us to the living Christ. Jesus gave us a commentary on the laws God gave to Moses.

Therefore, Bible Christians live (in word and deed) by the standards of the Bible, whereas worldly Christians set their *own standards* and try and make the Bible conform to their standards. An illusion that has deceived their hearts into believing that their standards will qualify them for the Kingdom of God which in God's reality it will not.

In contrast to worldly Christian belief, the law of Holiness and Judgment were written before the foundation of the world in the mind of God. The world would have God's people to believe that the requirement to enter the great city of God is for them only to "believe".

Accordingly, the belief that the world speaks of is a belief that gives ascent to God yet lacks obedience or reverence to God. This belief only requires the person to follow certain patterns of behavior. These patterns of behavior generated by this belief do not cause the person to make any distinction between him and the world when it comes to living for God.

As a result, this "world belief" has entered into the very fiber of the Church. It is perpetuated by those whose focus, is on the people and not God. I am not saying that we should not be concerned about people; however I am saying that people should not take priority over God. This is a devilish belief system, which has its origin from the very *annals of hell*. The bloodline runs from the father of this seed, Satan the great deceiver and contaminator of the world.

Satan gave birth to this belief system through two of his most deadly, life sucking, kings and nobles, the spirit of timidity and the spirit of cowardice. These spirits and their cohorts are at the very fiber of all unbelief, backsliding, and treason in the Kingdom of God. It is the catalysis used to destroy the vision given to God's people.

Furthermore, it not only destroys vision but it is the abortion pill for many mighty men and women of valor, who have aborted

God's plan for their lives, because they knowingly or unknowingly yield to this dreadful spirit of timidity and cowardice.

It is my aim, by the grace of the Holy Spirit, to reveal how the spirit of timidity and cowardice hinders and sometimes rules the lives of many of God's people. I will also show how this spirit goes unchecked in the lives of God's people and in the Church of God. The things revealed in the following pages will be difficult for the reader to accept, because it will cause the reader to confront him or herself. The reader will be forced to look through the lens and magnifying glass of God, the Holy Spirit.

It is not my goal to cover all the categories of spirits that are listed in the beginning of this chapter that will keep a person out of the kingdom of God. The scope of this book is limited to the spirit of timidity and the spirit of cowardice.

Since cowardice is the first category mentioned I believe that it is the foundation from which all the others originate and operate. It is my prayer that you, the reader, will allow the Holy Spirit to shine His light into every area of your life for the purpose of destroying the works of these spirits that oppose God and His children. He opposes God's children for the sole purposes of leading them into the lake of fire that burns with fire and brimstone.

Jesus provided victory over this enemy of God through His finished work at Calvary. The shedding of Jesus' precious blood at the cross *annihilated* the power of these spirits over the children of God. Will you receive your victory?

PRAYER:

Mighty and Glorious Father, God, I come to you under the precious blood of Jesus. I ask you to search me thoroughly and know my thoughts and reveal my heart to me. Open the eyes of my heart and flood it with light, so that I can know and understand the hope, to which You have called me. So that I may know and understand, the immeasurable, unlimited, and surpassing, greatness of Your power in and for me. I ask that you demonstrate Your mighty strength and love in my life. I ask that you enable me to come face to face with those things which are within me that are in defiance of You, Your Word, and Your plan for my life. Give me the strength and courage to come face to face, with myself and what you want me to understand, regarding the spirit of timidity and the spirit of cowardice. I trust you to show me. I ask this in the name of Jesus. Amen, so be it.

CHAPTER TWO

THE ORIGIN OF TIMIDITY AND COWARDICE
PART I

"Now the serpent was more subtle and crafty than any living creature of the field which the Lord God had made. And he (Satan) said to the woman, Can it really be that God has said, you shall not eat from every tree of the garden? (Rev.12: 9-11) And the woman said to the serpent, we may eat the fruit from the trees of the garden, except the fruit from the tree which is in the middle of the garden. God has said, you shall not eat of it, neither shall you touch it, lest you die. But the serpent said to the woman, you shall not surely die, (II Cor. 11:3.) For God knows that in the day you eat of it your eyes will be opened, and you will be like God, knowing the difference between good and evil and blessing and calamity. And when the woman saw that the tree was good (suitable, pleasant) for food and that it was delightful to look at, and a tree to be desired in order to make one wise, she took of its fruit and

ate; and she gave some also to her husband, and he ate." (Genesis 3:1-6)

This passage of Scripture describes Satan without his disguises. Yet, lets not forget that Satan *disguises* himself as an angel of light to the unsuspecting. He is a more subtle, wise, cunning, and crafty, (artful) than any living creature. Satan is called the adversary, devil, seducer, deceiver of all humanity, and the accuser of the brethren. (Rev 12:9-10)

"He was a murderer from the beginning and does not stand in the truth, because there is no truth in him. When he speaks falsehood he speaks what is natural to him, for he is a liar (himself) and the father of lies and of all that is false." (John 8:44)

In contrast to Satan, man was pure and undefiled as shown in the illustration below. Satan had absolutely nothing in man.

Satan has entered the Garden of Eden as a usurper and enemy of mankind. His aim in talking to Eve is to deceiver her in to handing over her authority to him so that he will become the ruler in her and Adam. The stage is set for the war of words.

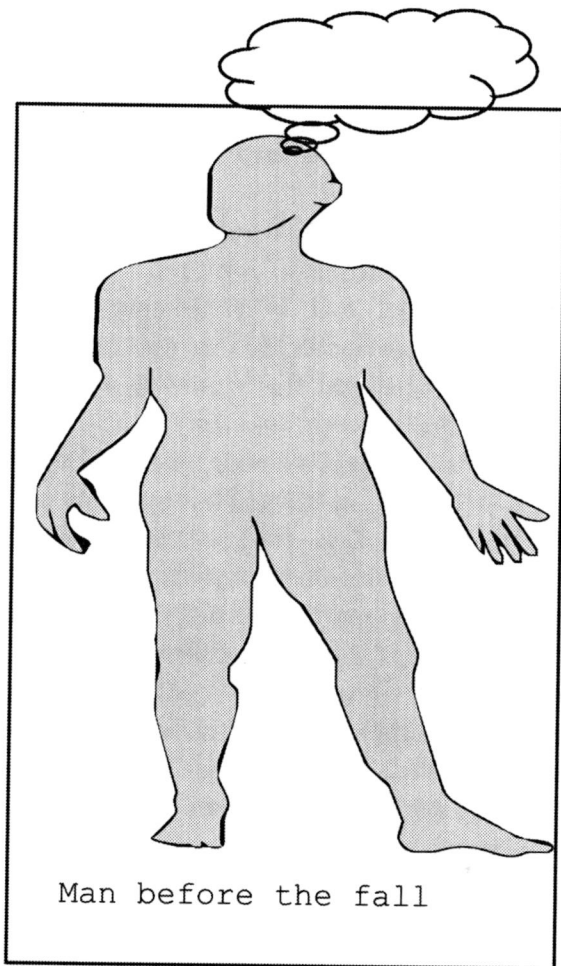

Man before the fall

"*A man's (moral) self shall be filled with the fruit of his mouth; and with the consequence of his words he must be satisfied (whether good or evil). Death and life are in the power of the tongue, and they who indulge in it shall eat the fruit of it (for death or life)" (Proverb 18:20-21 & Matt. 12:37)*

Satan was artful and cunning. Satan's plan was to fill Adam and Eve with *his* spiritual fruits. The way for him to accomplish this was to get them to accept the fruit of his lips, the words of his mouth. His goal was deceive (fruits) Eve, therefore deceiving Adam, because Adam and Eve were one in the spirit.

Eve was fully aware of her authority and her responsibility to obey God's command not to eat from the tree of knowledge of good and evil. When Satan called God a liar by saying, God knows that in the day you eat of the tree of knowledge of good and evil, that your eyes will be open and you will be like God. You will not truly die.

Again, Satan's goal was to impart his fruits to Adam and Eve. Satan *lied*, one of his fruits. Moreover, Satan knew the penalty for disobeying God. He knew that disobeying God would result in the spiritual and physical death to Adam and Eve, along with their expulsion from the Garden of Eden. He further knew that if Eve obeyed him instead of God, she would be relinquishing her delegated authority over to him.

Moreover, disobedience and rebellion are Satan's chief fruits. He had previously disobeyed God himself by rebelling against God and deceiving other members of the angelic host into following him. To Adam and Eve's demise, Satan's plan of imparting his fruits into their spirit and mind was successful. Eve ate the fruit and gave some to Adam.

Consequently man had not only relinquished his authority and accepted the nature of Satan; he had accepted the fruits of Satan's mouth, which spur forth immorality, iniquity, sin, death, and the fear of death. Am I saying humans are children of Satan, no, I am not, but I am saying that fallen humanity have certain attributes of Satan, such as, lying, rebellion, immorality, and cowardice (fruits of Satan). The fruit of Satan's mouth was spiritual death (separation from God) and physical death.

He imparted spiritual and physical death to both Adam and Eve, which still affects the entire human race. Satan also imparted his nature to Adam and Eve, which was later transmitted to their off springs.

In addition to taking on Satan's nature (fallen nature) man changed his bloodline from a divine bloodline of everlasting life and fellowship with the Almighty God to a bloodline of perverseness, and of destruction, flowing from Satan.

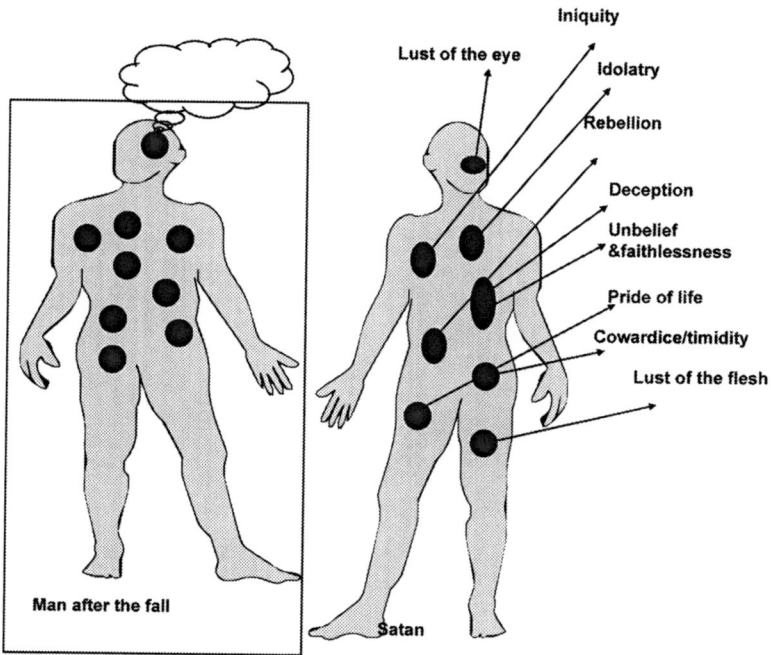

Man after the fall

Satan

Iniquity

Lust of the eye

Idolatry

Rebellion

Deception

Unbelief &faithlessness

Pride of life

Cowardice/timidity

Lust of the flesh

CHAPTER THREE

THE ORIGIN OF TIMIDITY AND COWARDICE PART II

"I will not talk with you much more, for the prince (evil, genius, ruler) of the world is coming. And he has no claim on Me. (He has nothing in common with Me; there is nothing in Me that belongs to him, and he has no power over Me.)" (John 14:30)

The tragic result of Satan's temporal victory over man was catastrophic. Man had accepted the fruits of Satan's mouth, which was an act of treason and rebellion against God. This treason and rebellion set in motion a cataclysmic reaction.

For example, man became spiritually dead, resulting in his separation from God. Man also began to die physically, meaning that he had lost his privilege of eternal life in the presence of God. Adam and Eve had relinquished their authority and dominion to govern God's creation on earth. Man's rebellion affected all creation.

Moreover, the animals that Adam named and cared for now became his *predator*. The earth that freely yielded his life food has now rebelled against him where he would have to toil with the sweat of his brow to feed himself. Adam and Eve's relationship had changed forever. They went from loving, cherishing, being, to blaming, accusing, and shifting, responsibility, being.

Subsequently, they became ashamed, proud, reluctant, and withdrawn from each other. Eve's desires shift from pleasing God, to pleasing Adam. Adam's desires shifted from pleasing God, to fending for food for survival. Instead of being partners, they became competitors.

Satan imparted and implanted immorality, iniquity, all forms of sin, all forms of perversion, all forms of sicknesses and diseases to Adam and Eve. Along with these things, Satan had imparted death and the fear of death.

Most tragically, Satan had conquered his nature was in man. He had something in man (humanity) that he could access any time he need to accomplish *his* will in man's life as well as man's off spring.

The illustration below shows man before the fall without any spots or blemishes. Man walked blameless before God and in complete fellowship with God. There was nothing in man that separated him from the presence of God and his relationship with God.

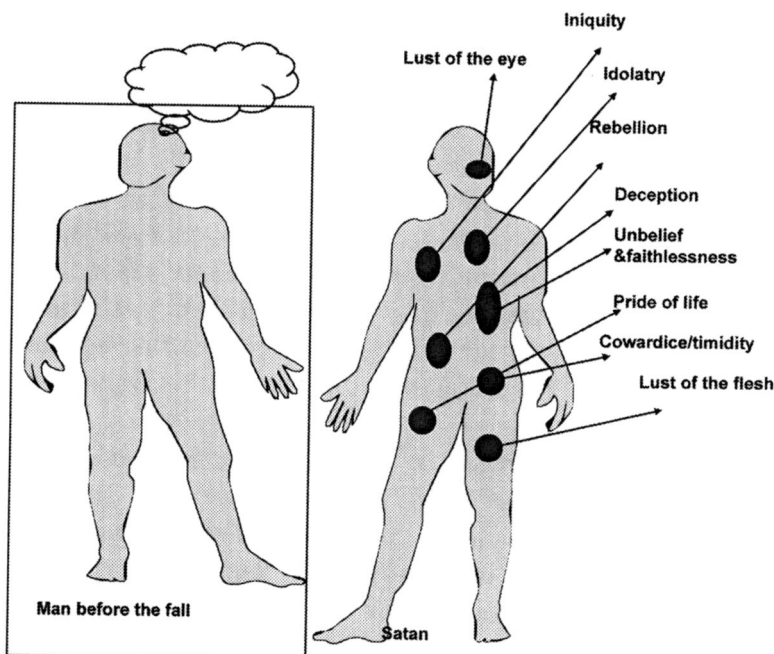

Iniquity
Lust of the eye
Idolatry
Rebellion
Deception
Unbelief &faithlessness
Pride of life
Cowardice/timidity
Lust of the flesh
Man before the fall
Satan

"I will not talk with you much more, for the prince (evil genius, ruler) of the world is coming. And he has no claim on Me. (He has nothing in common with Me; there is nothing in Me that belongs to him, and he has no power over Me.)" (John 14:30)

Adam and Eve blameless, just as Jesus was blameless. For example, Jesus told His disciples that the evil genius, ruler of the world, has no claim on Him. That the evil genius had nothing in common with Him; there is nothing in Him that belongs to the evil one and that the evil genius had no power over him.

Satan had no power over Jesus because there was nothing, absolutely nothing that he could claim in Jesus. Satan could not claim disobedience, rebellion, sin, iniquities, treason, cowardice, or perversion in Jesus. These things were not a part of Jesus' nature.

In Matthew chapter four Jesus was led into the desert/ wilderness to be tempted, tried, and tested by the devil. When the devil tempted Jesus, his goal was to impart his nature into Jesus, thereby, giving him access to Jesus. Jesus used the Word of God on Satan and defeated the devil.

In contrast, Adam and Eve were tested with the temptation of the devil, yet they failed their test and the result of their disobedience, was iniquities and separation from God.

"But your iniquities have made a separation between you and your God, and your sins have hidden His face from you, so that He will not hear. For your hands are defiled with blood and your fingers with iniquity; your lips have spoken lies, your tongue mutters wickedness. None sues or calls in righteousness (but for the sake of doing injury to others—to take some undue advantage); no one goes to law honestly and pleads (his case) in truth; they trust in emptiness, worthlessness, and futility, and speaking lies! They conceive mischief and bring forth evil! They hatch adders' eggs and weave the spider's web; he who eats of their eggs dies, and (from an egg) which is crushed a viper breaks out (for their nature is ruinous, deadly, evil).

Their webs will not serve as clothing, nor will they cover themselves with what they make; their works are works of iniquity, and the act of violence is in their hands. Their feet run to evil, and they make haste to shed innocent blood. Their thoughts are thoughts of iniquity; desolation and destruction

are in their paths and highways. The way of peace they know not, and there is no justice or right in their goings. They have made them into crooked paths; whoever goes in them does not know peace." (Rom. 3:15-18.) (Isaiah 59:2-8)

Isaiah paints a vivid picture of what took place in the interaction between Eve and the serpent. Eve chose to trust the serpent's words over God's words. The words (sperm/seed) she believed and received from the serpent conceived in her and brought forth evil.

She in turn infected Adam with this evil. The words the serpent spoke to Eve were adder eggs. Adam and Eve ate them and died. They ate eggs from which a viper broke forth and the nature of the viper was ruinous, deadly and evil.

The web that was woven over them removed their clothing of the glory of God. The works (of their offspring) became acts of violence and their feet ran to do evil (Cain kills Abel). Their thoughts were thoughts of iniquity, desolation, and destruction (Gen. chapter six).

Consequently, the way of peace they knew not. They had made their paths into crooked paths and these paths were filled with destruction.

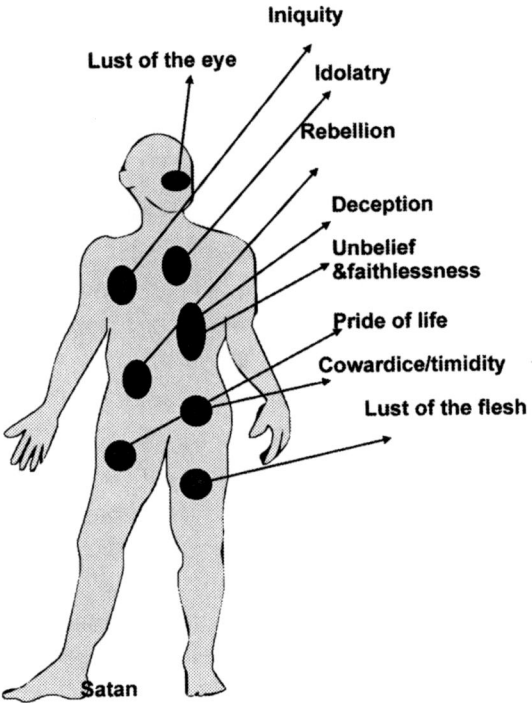

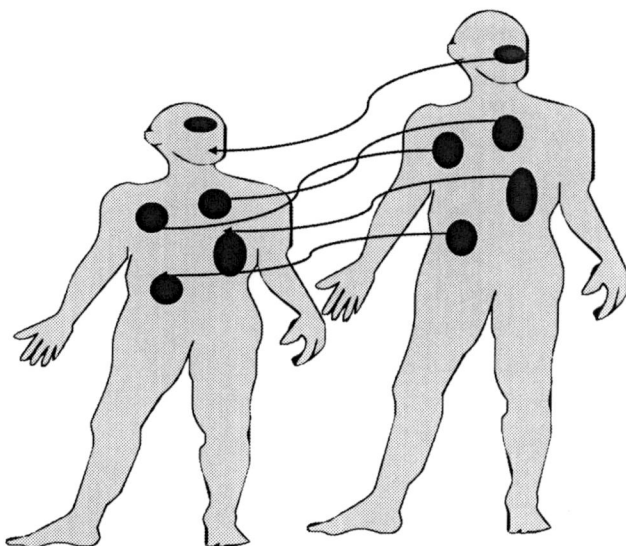

> *"A man's (moral) self shall be filled with the fruit of his mouth; and with the consequence of his words he must be satisfied (whether good or evil). Death and life are in the power of the tongue, and they who indulge in it shall eat the fruit of it (for death or life)."*
>
> *(Proverb 18:20-21)*

Eve ate the fruit of her lips as well as the fruits of the serpent's lips. The tongue has life and death in it. Eve could have used the life giving power of her tongue to counter the death giving power of the serpents tongue, but she did not. She submitted to the lies of the serpent and by doing so she indulged in the fruits of Satan's tongue, which resulted in death for, her and Adam, as well as humanity.

Although things looked dim for humanity, God had established a reconciliation plan before the foundation of the world. All was not lost for humanity. As we shall see in the following pages, but for now I want to define timidity and cowardice as defined in the word of God.

CHAPTER FOUR

WHAT IS THE TIMIDITY AND THE COWARDICE

⬧

"For God did not give us a spirit of timidity (of cowardice, of craven and cringing and fawning fear), but (He has given us a spirit) of power and of love and of calm and well-balanced mind and discipline and self-control."

(2 Timothy 1:7)

The Word of God clearly states that timidity and cowardice is a spirit. When God created man, He created man in His image and His likeness. Man was given dominion over all things that lived on the earth. Adam and Eve, the father and mother of all generations, rule the earth in faithfulness and courage. It was not until the fall of man that this spirit entered into the mind of Adam and Eve.

However, I will explain this statement later in this chapter, but first I will define timidity and cowardice as it is revealed in the Word of God. This can be accomplished by looking at the following Scripture again.

"For God did not give us a spirit of timidity (of cowardice, of craven and cringing and fawning fear), but (He has given us a spirit) of power and of love and of calm and well-balanced mind and discipline and self-control."

(2 Timothy 1:7)

Timidity and Cowardice is Satan's perversion of the strength and courage that God created in man. An example of this perversion of man's strength and courage before the fall of man is the suicide bomber.

It is widely known that on September 11, 2001, four planes were hijacked. Two crashed into the World Trade Center, one into the Pentagon, and the other crashed into the Pennsylvania countryside. It is said that nearly 3,000 people were killed by what is know as the weapon of choice for Islamic *Jihads*. These *Jihads* were the terrorist weapon; now wildly know as the "suicide bomber." It is said that in November 2005 insurgents in Iraq killed 7,611 people. 892 of these people were killed by suicide bombers.

It is also said that in Israel, from 1993 through March 2004 over 139 suicidal-attacks attributed to the Intifada of Palestine. More than 112 suicide bombings accounted for 474 of 918 Israeli deaths during this period. During this same period more than 3,000 Israeli's were wounded from suicide bombing attacks.

Many psychologists are tying to determine what type of human being this is that would attach bombs to themselves and blow themselves up along with hundreds of other people. The suicide bomber is not limited to gender or age. They come in all genders and all ages. *"The thief cometh not but to steal, kill, and destroy." (John 10:10)*

Suicide bombers are deceived and blinded human beings being used as agents of Satan. They, like Judas, has allowed Satan to blind their eyes and entice them to do ungodly and heinous things that Satan has deceived them into thinking is right and honorable. Satan blinds their eyes where they think that suicide is courage, when in all actuality, it is not courage, it is cowardice in its most heinous form.

Now back to the definition of timidity and cowardice. First, the word *spirit* in the original Hebrew text is *pneuma*. (4151) *Pneuma* means wind, breath, the spirit like the wind, is invisible, immaterial, and powerful. When speaking of humans, it is the rational soul, the vital principle, and mental disposition. When referring to a superhuman being, it is referring to an angel, demon, or the divine. When speaking of the divine, it is referring to God, Jesus Christ's spirit, and the Holy Spirit.

On the contrary, God is not speaking of the human spirit, the vital principle, and mental disposition of a man here, nor is he referring to His divine Spirit or His Son, Jesus the Anointed One. In this passage of Scripture, 2 Timothy 1:7 Paul is conveying to Timothy that *God has not* given us (people) a spirit of timidity and cowardice.

Accordingly, Paul is saying that the spirit of timidity and the spirit of cowardice come from a supernatural source *other* than God. This leaves one other source or origin for these spirits to come from. We must understand that these spirits are entities that are supernatural and invisible entities and originate from Satan. They are spirit beings seen only in the spirit world by spiritual eyes (the spirit of discernment).

Secondly, the types of spirits can be understood by defining the terms Paul used to describe the types of spirits mentioned in his discourse. The following definitions will be helpful in describing these spirits.

The word used in 2 Timothy 1:7, is *fearful*. It is the Greek word *deilia*, (1168) which means timidity, fearfulness, and cowardice. The derivates of deilla is deilo, (1169) to shrink for fear, and its adjective use is, fearful, and timid. It is always used in a bad sense such as *phobos,* which means, to flee or run away from.

In Hebrew, the word *fear* is *Yare* (3373), which means, fearing, being afraid, anxious, timid, or reverent. Its root is the word *Yare* (3372) which means, to be afraid, to rear, to revere, to be feared, to be dreadful, to be reverenced, to terrify, to make afraid. This word can be used in two ways, one to fear God and the other to fear something other than God.

I will be using the word in the manner of fearing someone or something other than God. In Hebrew the strong number for the word is 3372 and in Greek the Strong's number for the word is 1167 and 1169. By using the Strong's numbering system you can trace these words from the beginning of the Bible to the end of the Bible. Before proceeding it would be also helpful to define a few terms.

Coward/Cowardice - One showing ignoble fear in the face of danger or pain. A lack of courage or resoluteness.

Cowardly – Ignobly, dishonest, lacking in moral character, honor, generosity, lacking in courage, faint-hearted, chicken-hearted, craven, and yellow-bellied.

Craven - A coward, cowardly.

Cringing - To behave in a servile manner, to recoil, as in fear, fawn.

Fawn - To display obsequious affections. To seek favor supporting slavishly, every opinion and suggestion of a superior.

Fear - Alarm and agitation caused by the expectation or realization of danger. To be frightened, to be apprehensive about, to feel apprehensive.

Fearful - Causing or capable of causing fear, experiencing fear, frightened.

Noble - Having or displaying qualities of high moral character, as honor, generosity, or courage. Ignoble is the opposite of noble.

Shy - Easily startled, distrustful, lacking, to draw back, as from fear. A sudden movement, as from fright.

Timid - As to fear, shrinking from difficult or dangerous circumstances, fearful, shrinking from public attention.

I will only be discussing two terms, timidity and cowardice, with an emphasis on cowardice. Therefore, when using the word timidity, its meaning will be an inward entity/spirit or state of being that causes a person to shrink back from difficulties, pain, harm, or dangerous circumstances, resulting in a lack of courage, or resoluteness. The harm or danger may be real or imagined.

Cowardice encompasses the spirit of timidity. It is how a person responds to fear. Cowardice is thus, an inward or outward entity/spirit that deceives, oppresses, or possesses a person and causes that person to behave with a lack of courage or resoluteness. It causes a lack of moral character, honor, generosity, and courage, resulting in a person drawing back, fleeing, and or hiding from what the person perceives as danger, weather real or imagined. It not the self-protecting mechanism (fear) placed in man by God.

Cowardice is a spirit, which is a magnet for the agents of fear. It embeds itself in the mind and flesh of the *person,* therefore manifesting as part of the person's personality and character.

Whereas, fear is a response of the drawing of the inward or outward oppressive entity which deceives a person into thinking (soul) or feeling (emotions) and or *perceiving* as something as harmful or dangerous when it is not.

Furthermore, in a being, cowardly is the opposite of being courageous. God commands his servants-soldiers to be courageous and not to be timid and cowardly (Joshua 1:5-8). The spirit of cowardice, vehemently opposes the person God commands to be courageous, as well as the Word of God, that is within in the person. It is the servant of Satan, which opposes every form of might, courage, boldness, and valor in the men and women of God.

Finally, in 2 Timothy 1:7 we can make a distinction between the Spirit of God, His Holy Spirit and the spirits of Satan which tries to influence, oppress, or possess, believers as part of his assaults on the believers, who has received Jesus as Lord and Savior. Again, Paul informs Timothy that:

> **"God did** *not give us a spirit of timidity (of cowardice, of craven and cringing and fawning fear), but (He has given us a spirit) of power and of love and of calm and well-balanced mind and discipline and self-control. Do not blush or be ashamed then, to testify to and for our Lord, nor of me, a prisoner for His sake, but (with me) take your share of the suffering (to which the preaching) of the Gospel (may expose you, and do it) in the power of God."*
>
> *(1 Timothy 1:7-8)*

Spirit not given by God (Inward and or outward entity)	Spirit God gave Man (Inward state of being)
1. Spirit of timidity 2. Spirit of cowardice 3. Spirit of craven fear 4. Spirit of cringing fear 5. Spirit of fawning fear	1. Spirit of power=dunamis (1411) 2. Spirit of love=agapo (26) 3. Spirit of calm mind 4. Spirit of a well-balanced mind 5. Spirit of discipline 6. Spirit of self-control

From the chart you can clearly see six spirits that Paul mentions that God has given us through His Holy Spirit/the inward working and outward expression of the Holy Spirit. These spirits are like the spirit of faith mentioned when Paul states,

> *"Yet we have the same spirit of faith as he had who wrote, I have believed, and therefore have I spoken. We too believe, and therefore we speak." (2 Corinthians 4:13)*

In verse seven Paul tells Timothy, his son in the faith, that God did not give him a spirit of timidity and of cowardice. Therefore it is evident that the spirit of timidity and the spirit of cowardice are entities that are hindering Timothy from working fully in the ministry in which he has been called.

> *"Do not blush or be ashamed then, to testify to and for our Lord, nor of me, a prisoner for His sake, but (with me) take your share of the suffering (to which the preaching) of the Gospel (may expose you, and do it) in the power of God."*
> *(1 Timothy 1:7-8)*

These spirits were also causing Timothy to blush (to feel embarrassed) or ashamed (feeling guilt; reluctant through fear of shame). Why was Paul admonishing Timothy and why did he make a distinction between the Spirit of God and the spirits of timidity and cowardice.

I believe that Timothy was fully aware of the distinction between the three. Paul recognized that Timothy was under attack by these two spirits and that they were beginning to manifest themselves in Timothy's life affecting his walk with the Lord. Paul was encouraging Timothy to resist these spirits and to fight for the faith as a good soldier.

Paul had surely taught Timothy spiritual warfare and Timothy knew about spiritual warfare because he had accompanied Paul on part of his missionary journey.

As a result of the hardship on these missionary journeys Timothy had begun to buckle under the persecution as a result of the gospel. Timothy's spiritual father in the faith, Paul, had been imprisoned; most of those with Paul had deserted him for fear of being put into prison or they had turned away from walking with God (a very depressing situation).

Surely, Timothy knew these spirits had been unleashed on all the believers. Paul was conveying to Timothy that these spirits no longer have access to him, because Timothy was in Christ Jesus. Timothy was being exposed to the assault of the enemy of the Lord Jesus because he was preaching the gospel. These were territorial spirits hindering Timothy.

I was praying one morning around 4:00 A.M. and the Lord begin to describe the spirit of cowardice and timidity to me. As God began to describe these entities my spiritual eyes were open.

This vile spirit has two heads that both have eight half faces, four on each head. One head is shaped like the head of a dove and its four half faces are, the face of offense, the face of inordinate sensitivity, the face of whimpering, and the face of a baby with it features disfigured and retarded in growth.

The second head is a head of a dragon and its half faces are; the face is anger, the face of torment, the face of affliction, and the face of infirmity. These names are written on the top of the faces between the eyes.

The tongue is the same in both heads. It is a forked tongue. Its tongue sprays forth venom that paralyzes the mind and the body. This poison sprayed from its tongue contaminates its victims with its seeds of timidity and cowardice. This produces depression and fatigue in the person. Out of its mouth it breathes out the fire of slander, murder, war, aggression, passive aggression, dissension, discord, unbelief, faithlessness, idolatry, calamity, curses, and deafness.

It has two wings, which consist of feathers with words engraved on them. The right wing has hate, malice, vengeance cruelty, destruction, murder, and war. The left wing has engraved on it the words lies, accusation, perversion, mind control, isolation, retreating, unbelief, and faithlessness.

The wings enable this spirit to hover over people and places. Its feathers also have suction elements to suck up its prey while in flight or resting on something. The feathers in addition to having suction elements have tentacles that eject and attach to its prey and hold them captive while he devours its prey.

Its tail is long and wraps around it victims and squeezes the life out of them through suffocation and smothering them. There are feathers in it tail that has the words depression, heaviness, fatigue and slumber written on them.

Its claws enable it to clinch into the minds of men and the atmosphere binding them and controlling them to do its bidding. This spirit has a growl like a vicious wolf and when it growls an image of a wolf and fox appears. The spirit of timidity serves as a shadow for the spirit of cowardice. It is like a reflection of cowardice but it is not cowardice it is a distinct spirit apart from the spirit of cowardice.

The spirit of cowardice is flanked by the spirit of timidity, witchcraft, freemasonry, and eastern star (Isis). This spirit is a formable foe and is ranked with the spirit of Jezebel. Whenever you confront this spirit, you will have to war against its comrades (compos drays) freemasonry, eastern star, (Isis) witchcraft, and timidity.

Moreover, every believer who sincerely lives under the Lordship of Jesus Christ, will be exposed, attacked, and will war against these spirits. Surrendering to this spirit is suicidal. Its aim is death to all servant-soldiers.

PRAYER:

Father of Glory, mighty in power, awesome in wonders, merciful, and kind, I honor and glorify you. I come to you in the name and blood of Jesus, the Anointed One. I ask that you forgive me of my sins. I renounce the spirits of timidity and cowardice in my life. Through the power of the Holy Spirit and in the name and blood of Your Son Jesus Christ, I server all ties with these spirits, I bind them with chains and fetters of iron and I dislodge them from my life in the name and power of the blood of Jesus Christ. Father God, I thank you for opening my eyes to the works of these spirits and setting me free. I submit my life to the Holy Spirit to lead me and to teach me so that I will remain free. I thank you Father, for the finished work of the Cross, in my life in Jesus name. Amen. So be it.

CHAPTER FIVE

MILITARY DEFINITION OF COWARDICE

⸻

I served in the United States Army for over twenty years. I retired with an honorable discharge and a wealth of military experience. I was required to follow and adhere to the strict military discipline, laws, rules, and regulations. These military laws, rules, and regulations, govern every aspect of my life. It was mandatory that I was physically fit and technically and tactically proficient in my military occupation.

I was also required to be proficient with my assigned weapon. The military has a mandatory standard for physical fitness, occupational skills, and weapon mastery (You must qualify meaning you must meet a minimum standard).

Moreover, my only honorable escape from the military and its laws, was to leave the Army after faithfully fulfilling my contract of two-four years tours or retirement. Any other means of leaving the military carried with it the possibility of a dishonorable, less than honorable discharge, or some form of incarceration, neither of which interested me, therefore I retired with a smile.

However, before I retired, my life was governed by the Uniform Code of Military Justice, as are all soldiers in the Army regardless of rank or primary military occupation.

Whether in peace or combat these rules will govern the soldier's life. These laws range from the way a soldier speaks, to the way a soldier responds, to his or her superior. From the time a soldier takes the oath of office the soldier's life is controlled by his supreme commander down through the chain of command to his first line supervisor. The military has laws for both a time of peace and a time of war. I will discuss the law that governs cowardice.

First, let us re-look at who we are in Christ Jesus. We are both saints and soldiers. We suffer hardship and we should conduct our selves as soldiers in the Army of the Living God. We are to take what Paul said to Timothy as ours, not just some ink written on paper, to some saint in the early Church, no Paul is speaking to you and me.

>*"Take (with me) your share of the hardships and suffering (which you are called to endure) as a good (first-class) soldier of Christ Jesus. No soldier when in service gets entangled in the enterprises of (civilian) life; his aim is to satisfy and please the one who enlisted him. And if anyone enters competitive games, he is not crowned unless he competes lawfully (fairly, according to the rules laid down).*
>*(2 Timothy 2:3-4)*

The Word of God clearly states that we are soldiers of Christ Jesus and as such we should not get entangled with the affairs of civilian life. Our aim Beloved is to please the one who enlisted us, Jesus, the Captain of the Lord's Host.

In contrast to the worldly army, God's soldiers do not desert. There should be no desertion in God's Army. Unlike the soldiers that enlisted in the United States Army during World War II, "Over 21,000 military personnel were convicted and sentenced for desertion during the 3.5 years of the American involvement in World War II.

Of these 21,000, 49 were given the death penalty." According to the Pentagon, more than 5500 military personnel deserted in 2003-2004 following the Iraq invasion and occupation. The number is believed to have reached about 8000 by the first quarter of 2006. Another report stated that since the year 2000, about 40,000 troops from all branches of the military have deserted. (Wikipedia, the Free Online Encyclopedia).

Accordingly, as a soldier of Jesus Christ, the Captain of the Lord's Host, we are engaged in combat with His enemy. We are not and will not be exempt from combat duty nor will we have a life of rest and relaxation (R&R). The only rest we will find or have is **IN** Christ Jesus while we are engaged in His business being obedient to His command.

> *"As I looked, this horn made war with the saints and prevailed over them (Daniel 7:21) He (Satan) was further permitted to wage war on God's holy people (the saints) and to overcome them. And power was given him to extend his authority over every tribe and people and tongue and nation. (Satan inserted) (Revelation 13:7)*

Again, the Word of God establishes that all soldiers of Jesus Christ (saints, believers) are engaged in combat (war) against the enemy. If we are not engaged in the war (soldier) of God, then know this, a relentless war is being waged against us by the most evil and treacherous creatures of all times, Satan and his army. In other words, we are in a war regardless of whether we are an active participant or not.

Now let us discuss the military definition of cowardice. Under the United Army Uniform Cod of Military Justice, the maximum punishment for cowardice is the death penalty. Under military law cowardice can only be charged during a time war in an area of armed conflict. The maximum punishment for cowardice is the death penalty. Saints of God, we are in an armed conflict.

"As I looked, this horn made war with the saints and prevailed over them. (Daniel 7:21) He (Satan) was further permitted to wage war on God's holy people (the saints) and to overcome them. And power was given him to extend his authority over every tribe and people and tongue and nation. (Satan inserted) (Revelation 13:7)

THE MILITARY DEFINITION FOR COWARDICE CAN BE DEFINED AS

Running away from an enemy, willfully failing to do all within the soldier's power to fight or defend when it is his duty to do so, while in combat. Abandoning or surrendering any post or position that the soldier is tasked with defending. Willfully failing to do all within the soldier's power to fight or defend when it is his duty to do so, while in combat. Failing to arrive at the appointed place on time to deploy (or "move out") with their assigned unit, aircraft or ship is considered absence with out leave or AWOL). Endangering the safety of any post, position or area that the soldier is responsible for through disobedience, neglect or willful misconduct while in combat. The discarding of arms (weapons) or ammunitions while in combat. Refusing to give any needed aid or relief to fellow troops while in combat and performing other unspecified acts of "cowardly conduct" while in combat.

RUNNING AWAY FROM THE ENEMY

Refusing to accept that we are a solider of Jesus Christ and are in a battle is running away from the enemy. It is mentally running away from your enemy. The psychologist calls it denial. God call it cowardice.

For example, God has called us to be intercessor or to perform another duty in His kingdom. We are to busy with the cares of this life to perform these duties. We instead seek after wealth, and other material things. We feel that it is too difficult for us to be what God has called us to be. We are running away from both God and the enemy.

Oh but we may say that we attend Church every Sunday and Bible study on Wednesday evenings. No, we are punching our "We go to Church" ticket. As long as we are doing what we want to do and not what Jesus wants us to do, we are running away. And, I might add we are running the wrong way.

WILLFULLY FAILING TO DO ALL WITHIN THE SOLDIER'S POWER TO FIGHT OR DEFEND WHEN IT IS HIS DUTY TO DO SO WHILE IN COMBAT

"I have strength for all things in Christ Who empowers me (I am ready for anything and equal to anything through Him Who infuses inner strength into me; I am self-sufficient in Christ's sufficiency.) (Philippians 4:13)

Under the inspiration of the Holy Spirit, Paul said that God has equipped us to do all things in Christ Jesus and that we are equal to and ready for anything through Jesus Christ Who infuses us with inner strength (Philippians 4:13). Paul goes on to say that we are self-sufficient in Christ's sufficiency. Therefore, we will be without excuse.

Soldiers of the Cross, we cannot willfully fail to fight in this war against both God's enemy and ours. We must defend all the possessions and positions (blessings) that God has provided for us. We must defend our health and not let the enemy put sickness and disease on our body, which is God's temple. We cannot act cowardly in this regard. We must fight the good fight of a first class soldier.

ABANDONING OR SURRENDERING ANY POST OR POSITION THAT THE SOLDIER IS TASKED WITH DEFENDING

God has detailed or assigned every solder to a specific position/post with the mandate for His soldier to fully function in this office. God has equipped each of His soldiers to fulfill his or her assigned duty.

"And He raised us up together with Him and made us sit down together (giving us joint seating with Him) in the heavenly sphere (by virtue of our being) in Christ Jesus (the Messiah, the Anointed One.)"(Ephesians 2:6)

Jesus, the Captain of the Lord's Host, has raised us up together with Him and seated us in Him in heavenly places. Our position and post is in heavenly places. We are in a place of victory. We must never abandon the position that Jesus has given us. We must never surrender our position, nor our post Jesus has tasked us to defend. Jesus has tasked us to defend our rights and privileges as his saint-soldiers.

We must never, never, surrender or succumb to the enemy. We must walk and live in the grace provide to us by the finish work of the Cross. To abandon and fail to defend ourselves when the enemy wars against us with his blazing *lying* missiles of inadequacy, inferiority, slander, and rejection. We must not let Satan steal who we are in Jesus. We must, at all cost, defend our legal position in Christ Jesus.

We have a birthright, an inheritance that we must possess and help each other to possess. Jesus has provided the resources we need to defend it. We have lost souls that have been destined before the foundation of the world to be brought into God's kingdom by Jesus through us. We must not abandon the lost souls to the devil. We must defend these precious souls, "our post" through fervent prayer and constant intercession until the Great I Am relieves us of our post.

"Behold! I have given you authority and power to trample upon serpents and scorpions, and (physical and mental strength and ability) over all the power that the enemy (possesses); and nothing shall in any way harm you.

(Luke 10:19)

Beloved Soldiers of Jesus, Jesus has given us authority and power (physical and mental strength and ability) over **ALL** the power our enemy possesses. The enemy can do nothing to harm us if we would stand and defend ourselves against him. If we do any thing less than fight we are abandoning and surrendering our position of authority. We are surrendering our power to the enemy whose sole mission is to steal from us, to kill us, and to destroy us.

ENDANGERING THE SAFETY OF ANY POST, POSITION, OR AREA THAT THE SOLDIER IS RESPONSIBLE FOR THROUGH DISOBEDIENCE, NEGLECT, OR WILLFUL MISCONDUCT, WHILE IN COMBAT

Soldier of the Cross, we are responsible for our families (posts), homes, churches, communities, and cities (area). We endanger the safety of our families, our homes, our churches, our communities and our cities when we refuse to obey Jesus Christ and neglect to pray and to intercede for each of them.

Therefore, when God commands us to do something in His Word and we willfully fail to do it, it is dereliction of duty. The Holy Bible is God's manual of war, a life of war while on this earth. It is our responsibility to obey God.

DISCARDING ARMS (WEAPONS) OR AMMUNITION IN COMBAT

"Stand therefore (hold your ground), having tightened the belt of truth around your loins and having put on the breastplate of integrity and of moral rectitude and right standing with God, And having shod your feet in preparation (to face the enemy with the firm-footed stability, the promptness, and the readiness produced by the good news) of the Gospel of peace. Lift up over all the (covering) shield of saving faith, upon which you can quench all the flaming missiles of the wicked (one). And take the helmet of salvation and the sword that the Spirit wields, which is the Word of God."

(Eph 6:14-17)

Ephesians chapter 6 gives us instruction regarding our responsibility in combat. According to Ephesians 6:14-17 Paul tell us that our weapons are truth, integrity, moral rectitude, right standing with God, the Gospel of peace, saving faith, the Word of God, and ceaseless prayer (intercession).

Also in I Peter 4:1, Peter instructs us to arm ourselves with the same thoughts and purposes of Christ Jesus. These are the weapons and ammunition that we use against the enemy. Our flesh is no match for Satan and his cohorts. We must engage him with the weapons and ammunitions that have been supplied by El **Shaddai**, our All Sufficient One.

REFUSING TO GIVE ANY NEEDED AID OR RELIEF TO FELLOW TROOPS WHILE IN COMBAT

Refusing to give needed aid and relief to our fellow troops is one of the most prevalent forms of cowardice there is in the body of Christ. Failure to intercede for fellow believers (not just the ones in your particular fellowship) is failing to render aid and relief.

For example, a brother or sister is ill and needs our concerted prayer. We refuse to pray for them because we are too busy with the cares of this life. We failed to provide needed assistance. Failure to love one another as Jesus has commanded us to love is refusing to render first aid and relief.

For instance, we are aware that someone is hurting in our congregation from domestic violence, instead of showing them love we gossip about their situation. We have failed to apply our weapon of love against the enemy on behalf of this hurting person.

To look at it another way, when one of our loved ones is in bondage to some thing such as food, drugs, profanity, and the likes, we want them to stop. Yet we resent them for their shortcomings an inability to trust the Lord Jesus, however, we never spend time in fervent prayer for them and for their deliverance. We have failed to render first aid to this person.

Suppose God told one of us to quit our full time job, and get a part time job so that we could do more work for His kingdom. God's plan (that you don't know about) is to make us available for the souls that he is going to send to us to lead to salvation and to train as His disciple.

Our failure to respond to God's call is a failure to render first aid to the lost soul and relief to them by training them to be disciples of the Lord Jesus.

CHAPTER SIX

GOD'S ARMY

"Then Abimelech went to him from Gerar with Ahuzzah, one of his friends, and Phicol, his 'army's' commander. And Isaac said to them, why have you come to me, seeing that you hate me and have sent me away from you? They said, We saw that the Lord was certainly with you; so we said, Let there be now an oath between us (carrying a curse with it to befall the one who breaks it), even between you and us, and let us make a covenant with you That you will do us no harm, inasmuch as we have not touched you and have done to you nothing but good and have sent you away in peace. You are now the blessed or favored of the Lord! And he made them a (formal) dinner, and they ate and drank. And they rose up early in the morning and took oaths (with a curse) with one another; and Isaac sent them on their way and they departed from him in peace."
(Genesis 26:26-31 emphasis mine)

The word army is first mentioned in Genesis chapter twenty-six through thirty-one when it is used in conjunction with Abimelech, army commander.

Although Abimelech' army is not in the commonwealth of God's *chosen* people, Abimelech's army falls under Jehovah as part of God's army in the sense that, *"The earth is the Lord's and the fullness of it, the world and they who dwell in it."* (Psalm 24:1) The Hebrew word for army used in verse twenty-six is **tsaba or tseba'ah** (6633) pronounced **tsaw-baw or tseb-aw-aw.** It means, a mass of persons, especially regularly organized for war (an army); it also means battle, host, company, service, soldier, and waiting upon war.

In Genesis chapter twenty-six we see how God subdued Abimelech. For example, although Abimelech is hostile toward Isaac he wants to overt any future war with Isaac's and his people.

In contrast to Abimelech, Isaac trusted his God as his covenant partners. God let Isaac know that He is with him and that he would favor him with blessings. (Genesis 26:24) God established Himself as Isaac's defense against anyone or anything.

The Lord God Jehovah was Isaac's army and supreme army commander in the same way that he was Abraham's supreme army commander, as Abraham's covenant partner. In addition, Abimelech and Phicol, his army commander recognized that every time they tried to indirectly defeat Isaac they failed.

For example, Abimelech had asked Isaac to move from among them after he found out that Rebekah was Isaac's wife. Abimelech also allowed his people to confiscate several wells Isaac and his servant had dug, (water is the life line in this part of the world). (Genesis 26) Abimelech understood that Isaac's army was provided by Isaac's God. For fear of Isaac's God, Abimelech set up a meeting with Isaac to make a covenant. Abimelech brought the commander of his army while Isaac represented God's local army commander on the ground for Jehovah, the "Self–Existent One."

There are two other Hebrew words used for army. One is the word host. (Please note that army is a synonym for host). First, the Hebrew word for host is **macha-neh or makh-an-eh** (4264) which means an encampment (of travelers or troops); hence an army, whether literally (of soldiers) or figuratively (of dancers, angels, cattle, locusts, stars; or even the sacred courts.) It also means camp, company, drove, and tents.

The word **machaneh** or **makh-an-eh** speaks of an angelic army, the stars, sacred courts and certain forms of the animal kingdom, such as locus and cattle. When the word **machaneh** or **makh-an-eh** is used it can and often refers to spiritual host or celestial host.

GOD'S CELESTIAL ARMY

"Thus the heavens and the earth were finished, and all the host (machaneh or makh-an-eh) all of them. (Genesis 2:1)

Here God speaks about the stars, moon, the sun, and numerous celestial bodies that emit radiant energy, such as light and other luminous bodies that He has made. The creation of man is included in the hosts that are mentioned here in Genesis 2:1.

In 2 Kings 6:16-17, Elisha asked God to open the eyes of his young servant so that he may see that God had provided an army of his celestial being to protect and fight with and for Elisha, his prophet.

If only God's people would choose to believe that God is still willing to reveal His celestial army to His saints, to protect and do battle with them, in their fight against the enemy.

GOD'S ARMY OF ANGELS

"Then Jacob went on his way, and God's angels met him. When Jacob saw them, he said, This is God's army! So he named that place Mahanaim (two armies)." (Gen. 32:7, 10) (Genesis 32:1-2)

Clearly stated here in Genesis chapter 32:1-2, God has an angelic army that was visible to Jacob. Not only did Jacob see God's angelic armies, Jacob named the place where he saw God's angelic host the place of **Mahanaim**. Glory to God!

We are heirs and joint-heirs with Jesus Christ therefore we have armies of angels ready to do our bidding in fulfilling the plans and purposes of God in His Church and in our lives.

The second word for host is the Hebrew word **chayil** pronounced **khah'-yil. (2428)** It means a force, resources, an army, wealth, virtue, valor, and strength. It further means able, activity, army, band of men (soldiers), company, (great) forces, goods, host, might, power, riches, strong, substance, train, valiant, valiantly, valor, virtuous, virtuously, war, worthy, and worthily.

"I will harden (make stubborn, strong) Pharaoh's heart, that he will pursue them, and I will gain honor and glory over Pharaoh and all his host (chayil), and the Egyptians shall know that I am the Lord. And they did so." (Exodus 14:4)

Host in Exodus 14:4 describes Pharaoh's army. Pharaoh's host includes his might, resources, substance, as well as his power and riches.

His host also includes, his power and his riches. The army of Pharaoh protected Pharaoh's power, resources, substance, and riches. Jehovah had already executed judgment against Pharaoh's gods by smiting them (rendering them power-less) during the night the destroyer killed both the first-born humans and the first born of all beasts of the Egyptians.

"And the Angel of God Who went before the host (machaneh or makh-an-eh) of Israel moved and went behind them; and the pillar of the cloud went from before them and stood behind them, Coming between the host (machaneh or makh-an-eh) of Egypt and the host (machaneh or makh-an-eh) of Israel. It was a cloud and darkness to the Egyptians, but it gave light by night to the Israelites; and the one host (machaneh or makh-an-eh) did not come near the other all night."
(Exodus 14:19-20)(Hebrew insert is mine)

Again, the Hebrew word used here describes both the army of Israel and Pharaoh. What is amazing about this is that God put a barrier between Pharaoh's army and the army of Israel. The barrier (cloud by day and pillar of fire by night) was the Israelites guide and protection from their enemies. It was a weapon of darkness and hindrance for the Egyptians. God always draws a line of distinction between His people and their enemies.

GOD'S HUMAN AND CELESTICAL ARMIES

"When Joshua was by Jericho, he looked up, and behold, a Man stood near him with His drawn sword in His hand. And Joshua went to Him and said to Him, Are you for us or for our adversaries? And He said, No (neither), but as Prince of the Lord's host (tsaba or tseba'ah) have I now come. And Joshua fell on his face to the earth and worshiped, and said

to Him, What says my Lord to His servant? And the Prince of the Lord's host (tsaba or tseba'ah) said to Joshua, Loose your shoes from off your feet, for the place where you stand is holy. And Joshua did so. (Exodus. 3:5) (Joshua 5:13-15)

Jesus, the Prince, Captain of the Lord's host, paid Joshua, His earthly General, a visit to encourage him. It is not stated what the Prince of the Lord's Host conveyed to Joshua during His visitation with Joshua. However, we do know that the words he used, "Loose your shoes from off your feet, for the place where you stand is holy," are the same words that was spoken to Moses prior to Moses' was commissioned to go to Egypt to deliver the Israelites.

During the entire course of Joshua's conquest of the Promise Land, the Lord God fought for him. The celestial host fought for Joshua when the sun stood still. Jehovah's supernatural host under the command of Jehovah crushed the wall of Jericho. Bless Jehovah Tsaba the Lord of Armies!

CHAPTER SEVEN

THE DIFFERENCE BETWEEN GOD'S ARMY AND SATAN'S ARMIES

God's armies are commanded by the Captain of the Lord's Host, Jesus Christ the Lamb that was slain before the foundation of the world. All of God's soldiers volunteer. They volunteer to give their lives for their Commander and Chief. They are called in to a holy service of bondservants, whose sole mission is to obey the Captain of the Lord Host, in every aspect of the war and battle in defeating the enemy.

Arrayed in the armor of God, these armies fight from a position of victory. They are dressed in righteousness. Shielded by God's glory and armed with the Sword of the Spirit, (Word of God), the Gospel of Peace, the Shield of Faith, and the Garment of Praise.

Their weapons are not carnal, but mighty through the pulling downs of strongholds. (2 Corinthians 10:3-5) They know no retreat, and their battle cry is forward, El Shaddai, forward. Their offense is agape love, concerted intercession, praise, and daily repentance.

God's armies, take counsel from their Supreme Commander and from His counselors. Their minds are conditioned to fight like David fought by saying what David said and doing what David did as seen in the I Samuel chapter seventeen.

"And David said to the men standing by him, What shall be done for the man who kills this Philistine and takes away the reproach from Israel? For who is this uncircumcised Philistine that he should defy the armies of the living God? (I Samuel 17:26) Then said David to the Philistine, You come to me with a sword, a spear, and a javelin, but I come to you in the name of the Lord of host, the God of the ranks of Israel, Whom you have defied. This day the Lord will deliver you into my hand, and I smite you and cut off your head. And I will give the corpses of the army of the Philistines this day to the birds of the air and the wild beasts of the earth, that all the earth may know there is a God in Israel. And all this assembly shall know that the Lord save not with sword and spear; for the battle is the Lord's, and He will give you into our hands. When the Philistine came forward to meet David, David ran quickly toward the battle line to meet the Philistine David put his hand into his bag took out a stone and slung it, and it struck the Philistine, sinking into his forehead, and he fell on his face to the earth. So David prevailed over the Philistine with a sling and with a stone, and struck down the Philistine and slew him. But no sword was in David's Hand. So he ran and stood over the Philistine, took his sword and drew it out of its sheath, and killed him, and cut off his head with it. When the Philistines saw that their mighty champion was dead, they fled." (1 Samuel 45-51)

God's armies recognize that they serve a God that cannot fail. Their God fights for them. Their God destroy giants and routes all enemy armies. Oh Soldiers of the cross, if we would only reach into our bag. Our spirit is infused with the Spirit of the living God. The Holy Spirit pulls out the stone (the power of God) from our bag to destroy our enemies.

Oh what a God! Oh what a commander that commands His army in war, kills Goliaths, feeds their enemy's flesh to the birds of the air, and the wild beasts of the field. He routes their armies making them retreat in utter shame and defeat. This is Jehovah, the Lord of Host, and we are His armies.

In total contrast to God's armies, Satan's army is shrouded in darkness and cloaked in wickedness. Satan's army's offense is lies and deception to unsuspecting souls chained and blinded by his falsehood.

His most effective offensive weapon is the spirit of cowardice that masquerades itself as a dove but is really a vicious fire-expelling dragon. This ferocious demon has two heads, one camouflaged as of a dove that projects gentleness, kindness, fragility, and sensitivity. While the other, a dragon which is a predator that lurks in the dark to destroy those deceived by the devilish dove that masquerades as a gentle angel.

The defenses of the devil's army are: Accusation, slander, lust of the eye, lust of the flesh, and the pride of life. Satan's arsenal is filled with weapons of iniquity, idolatry, rebellion, desertion, dereliction of duty, unbelief, faithlessness, timidity, sorcery, and uncircumcised hearts.

Also, Satan's armies fight from a position of defeat; God Himself kicked his armies out of heaven. The devil and his army's have been defeated by the Captain of the Lord of Host.

"(God) disarmed the principalities and powers that were ranged against us (God's armies) and made a bold display and public example of them, in triumphing over them in Him and in it (the cross)." (Colossians 2:15) "Which He exerted in Christ when He raised Him from the dead and seated Him at His (own) right hand in heavenly (places). Far above all rule and authority and power and dominion and every name that is named (above every title that can be conferred), not only in this age and in this world, but also in the ages sand the world which are to come. And He has put all things under His feet and has appointed Him the universal and supreme Head of the church (a headship exercised throughout the church." (Psalm 8:6) (Ephesians 1:21-22)

Satan's armies are defeated and there is no victory in them. His armies can only win when God's army surrenders. Dear Beloved, we should never surrender to defeat when our Commander, Jesus Christ, has already won all wars and all battles that can be fought and legally positioned us in a place of eternal victory with Him.

CHAPTER EIGHT

GOD'S SERVANT-SAINT-SOLDIER

The word *soldier* in the United States provokes an image in the mind, of an American soldier in Iraq or Afghanistan, in combat uniforms with weapons in his hands and a Nuclear, Biological and Chemical (NBC) Protective Mask, striped to their sides or the images of coffins with the American flag draped over it, carried by soldiers in Class A uniforms.

In addition to these images are the thoughts of soldiers fighting, dying, being wounded, and suffering from some type of combat related Post Traumatic Stress Syndrome. These are considered natural occurrences for soldiers engaged in combat.

Also, it would be considered foolish as well as dangerous and deadly for a soldier to go to war without being trained: having proper leadership, (Military Commander) having the proper gear, and having the proper weapon. Citizens of our nation would think it was criminal to send soldiers off to war without everything they needed for their protection, in hope of their safe return to their families. Comrades, would God do less for His soldiers? No certainly not.

ENLIST FOR SERVICE

A soldier is someone who enlisted or is drafted into the armed forces of it nations. The soldiers are required to be loyal and obedient to the military laws that govern them in peace and in war times. The word soldier is a synonym for warrior, fighter, or combatant.

Unlike the American soldiers or natural human soldiers, God's soldier is not just a mere human. God's soldiers are a supernatural beings, created in the image and likeness of God. God's soldier enlists in God's army by swearing allegiance to Jesus Christ.

In addition to swearing allegiance to Jesus, he takes an oath of office that declares that he believes Jesus Christ came in the flesh, died on the cross, was resurrected from the dead, and now sits at the right hand of God the Almighty and absolute Sovereign Redeemer. (Romans 10:9-11)

Based on this oath the soldier has committed to being an over-comer by the blood of Lamb (Jesus), and the words of his testimony, that he or she will love Jesus more than he loves his own life. (Revelation 12:11)

Moreover, God's soldiers are sacred soldiers. They are wholly consecrated and dedicated to God. They do not entangle themselves in the affairs to this world, but they live their lives under total submission to Jesus, their Commander-in-Chief. *These soldiers are holy men and women of war.*

They know their God as Moses and the Israelites knew their God. They know Him as, "The Lord is my Strength and my Song, and He has become my Salvation; this is my God, and I will praise Him, my father's God, and I will exalt Him. *The Lord is a Man of War*; the Lord is His name." (Exodus 15:2-3)

ASSIGNED SPECIFIC DUTY IN SPECIFIC PLACES

In God's Word we find examples of His soldiers. We do well to study their example and the standards that God required them to follow. Below are several examples of the type of soldiers who where enlisted in God's mighty army.

"AFTER THE death of Moses the servant of the Lord, the Lord said to Joshua son of Nun, Moses' minister, (Deut. 34:4-8.) Moses My servant is dead. So now arise (take his place), go over this Jordan, you and all this people, into the land, which I am giving to them, the Israelites. Every place upon which the sole of your foot shall tread, that have I given to you, as I promised Moses. From the wilderness and this Lebanon to the great river Euphrates—all the land of the Hittites (Canaan)— and to the Great (Mediterranean) Sea on the west shall be your territory. No man shall be able to stand before you all the days of your life. As I was with Moses, so I will be with you; I will not fail you or forsake you." (Joshua 1:1-5)

The first thing that God do with his soldier Joshua is to call him by name. God do not give his soldiers social security numbers. He knows them personally. He knows everything about them. He knows their names and He calls them by name.

Secondly, God addresses Joshua by title, by his position, and by what position Joshua is to function in. He lets Joshua know that He is the one that set him in the position and conferred the title on him.

Thirdly, the Lord commands Joshua to, *"arise and take your place"*. (Joshua 1:2) The word arise is the Hebrew word is *quwm, (6965)* pronounced *koom* it means to abide, accomplish, be clearer, confirm, continue, decree, endure, enemy, enjoin (command), get up, make good, help, hold, lift up, build, newly ordain, perform, remain, be stable, stand, stir up, strengthen, succeed, and make good.

Beloved, God used one word, *quwm,* to speak into Joshua's being and create everything that He wanted him to be and do. Beloved, when God speaks to us, He's speaking tremendous things into our being. When God, our Almighty, All Sufficient One, calls us to do something when He speaks, *it is completed in us at that very moment.*

Moreover, it is settled in heaven and on earth and no demon in hell or anything else can stop it unless we, Soldier of the Cross, allow him to stop us. God tells us in Jeremiah 1:19, that the enemy will fight against us but he will not overcome us. Glory to God!

EMPOWERED BY THE WORKS OF HIS GOD, JEHOVAH

"Be strong (confident) and of good courage, for you shall cause this people to inherit the land which I swore to their fathers to give them. Only you be strong and very courageous, that you may do according to all the law which Moses My servant commanded you. Turn not from it to the right hand or to the left, that you may prosper wherever you go. This Book of the Law shall not depart out of your mouth, but you shall meditate on it day and night, that you may observe and do according to all that is written in it. For then you shall make your way prosperous, and then you shall deal wisely and have good success. Have not I commanded you? Be strong, vigorous, and very courageous. Be not afraid, neither be dismayed, for the Lord your God is with you wherever you go."   *(Joshua 1:6-9)*

A Soldier of God causes God's people to inherit what God has given them (if the people are willing to follow God's soldier). In the verses above, God is speaking into Joshua's being. These are not just words spoken in the air. These are creative words of the Almighty God.

These are accomplishing words, non-failing words, of the Almighty, sent as spirit agents of God into Joshua's spiritual man to effectually work out what God is commanding him to do. When God said be strong. Strong *became* in Joshua. When God said be courageous, *courage* became in Joshua.

Yes, Joshua had these attributes, which is apparent when he served under Moses. Yet, now God has given Joshua, His courage for the mission, that He was giving him. God has given Joshua, His strength for the mission that He was commissioning him for.

Not only was God speaking courage and strength into Joshua's being, but God was also speaking vigor into Joshua. The words that God spoke to Joshua imparted energy to do the will of God, vitality to endure what he had to face, drive to keep his face set toward the goal, and force to lead God's people and defeat his enemies.

FIGHT IN THE UNSEEN AND INVISIBLE WORLD

"Then Joshua spoke to the Lord on the day when the Lord gave the Amorites over to the Israelites, and he said in the sight of Israel, Sun, be silent and stand still at Gibeon, and you, moon, in the Valley of Ajalon! And the sun stood still, and the moon stayed, until the nation took vengeance upon their enemies. Is not this written in the Book of Jasher? So the sun stood still in the midst of the heavens and did not hasten to go down for about a whole day. There was no day like it before or since, when

the Lord heeded the voice of a man. For the Lord fought for Israel." (Joshua 10:12-14)

God's men and women of war (soldiers) have the ability through the power of the Holy Spirit to look into and operate in the unseen and invisible world. I would like to give you a glimpse into the invisible world of Joshua and the people of Israel in their battle with the Amorites.

"For I will pass through the land of Egypt this night and will smite all the firstborn in the land of Egypt, both man and beast; and against all the gods of Egypt I will execute judgment (proving their helplessness). I am the Lord." (Exodus 12:12)

Just as God told Moses in Exodus 12:12, God had given Joshua a mandate to destroy the Canaanite nations. As with Moses, when God delivered the Israelites from Egypt, he executed judgment on the nation's gods, demonic forces in the cosmos, which try to control the celestial bodies, such as the stars, moon, sun, and other celestial bodies, to hinder the work of God.

What we see going on here is not just a battle or a war between human forces (armies) this is a war between the demonic supernatural powers that oppose God and His people.

Moreover, Joshua had requested divine intervention in the heavens surrounding the moon and the sun. The gods of the Amorites such as, Marduk and his cohorts (the five nations) were opposing Joshua and the Israelites. God gave Joshua power over the demonic forces opposing him. When Joshua commanded the moon and the sun to stand, still he bound the demonic powers that where manipulating bodies in the cosmos to work against him.

For example, when Jesus was asleep in a boat on the Galilean sea with His disciples, the devil used comic forces to try and kill them. A terrible storm arose that threatened the life of Jesus and His disciples. What did Jesus do?

"And a furious storm of wind (of hurricane proportions) arose, and the waves kept beating into the boat, so that it was already becoming filled. But He (himself) was in the stern (of the boat), asleep on the (leather) cushion; and they awoke Him and said to Him, Master, do You not care that we are perishing? And He arose and rebuked the wind and said to the sea, Hush now! Be still (muzzled)! And the wind ceased (sank to rest as if exhausted by its beating) and there was (immediately) a great calm (a perfect peacefulness)." (Mark 4:37-39 emphasis mine)

What a God we serve. God's men and women of war are aware of the awesome power that God has infused them with to defend themselves and others in the kingdom of God.

PRAYER:

God, help your people to hear and receive Your Word so that Your Word will do what You sent it to do in their lives. Father, teach us, who You are and how to live in the seat, where you have position us, in Jesus Christ, our Savior and Lord. We are in need of this knowledge throughout Your Body, the Glorious Church. We need this revelation in this hour, dear God. Do not hold it back. Release it to your Church, oh wonderful Father, in Jesus' name. Amen. So be it.

THE CREED OF GOD'S SOLDIERS

"He who dwells in the secret place, of the Most High, shall remain stable and fixed under the shadow of the Almighty (Whose power, no foe can withstand). I will say of the Lord, He is my Refuge and my Fortress, my God; on Him, I lean and rely, and in Him, I (confidently) trust! For (then) He will deliver you from the snare of the fowler and from the deadly pestilence. (Then) He will cover you with His pinions, and under His wings shall you trust and find refuge; His truth and His faithfulness are a shield and a buckler. You shall not be afraid of the terror of the night, nor of the arrow (the evil plots and slanders of the wicked) that flies by day, Nor of the pestilence that stalks in darkness, nor of the destruction and sudden death that surprise and lay waste at noonday. A thousand may fall at your side, and ten thousand at your right hand, but it shall not come near you. Only a spectator shall you be (yourself inaccessible in the secret place of the Most High) as you witness the reward of the wicked. Because you have made the Lord your refuge, and the Most High your dwelling place, (Ps. 91:1, 14) There shall no evil befall you, nor any plague or calamity come near your tent. For He, will give His angels (especial) charge over you, to accompany and defend and preserve you in all your ways (of obedience and service). They shall bear you up on their hands, lest you dash your foot against a stone. (Luke 4:10, 11; Heb. 1:14) You shall tread upon the lion and adder; the young lion and the serpent shall you trample underfoot. (Luke 10:19.) Because he has set his love upon Me, therefore will I deliver him; I will set him on high, because he knows and understands My name (has a personal knowledge of My mercy, love, and kindness—trusts and relies on Me, knowing I will never forsake him, no, never). He shall call upon Me, and I will answer him; I will be with him in trouble, I will

deliver him and honor him. With long life will I satisfy him and show him My salvation." (Psalm 91 entire chapter)

CHAPTER NINE

SOLDIER'S AUTHORITY
IS DELEGATED AUTORITY

⤙⤚

In order to understand the operations of the spirit of timidity and the spirit of cowardice, we must become aware of the authority and the order of authority in God's kingdom. God created man to rule over his handiworks and to have fellowship with Him. Man was God's most prized possession. His desire for man was dominion and ruler-ship over *His* creation.

> *"And God blessed them and said to them, be fruitful, multiply, and fill the earth, and SUBDUE it (using all its vast resources in the service of God and man); and have DOMINIOM over the fish of the sea, the birds of the air, and over every living creature that moves upon the earth."*
> *(Genesis 1:28)(Emphasis mine)*

God created man with an innate ability to rule over creation. Man had the very life of God in him. Adam and Eve were God's very own children, created in His image and likeness, empowered as agents with volition, the right to choose and make decisions. (Genesis 1:26)

Elohim set man up as the king of the earth with all the power to enforce God's government on earth. Adam and Eve were not only ambassadors on the earth for Elohim; they were His governing body (authority). For example, in Genesis 1:28, Elohim gave Adam and Eve dominion over the fish of the sea, the birds of the air, and over every living creature that moved upon the face of the earth. God gave a warning signal, which enables man to sense impending danger.

Consequently, Adam and Eve's dominion encompassed every thing that moved on the earth. That included spiritual beings and physical beings. If a spiritual being came to the earth and moved within the earth's atmosphere Adam and Eve had dominion over it.

Why did Adam and Eve have dominion over any *thing* that came within the sphere or zone of the earth? He had this dominion because God delegated this authority to him as seen in Genesis 1:28.

Moreover, if the wind moved on the earth, Adam and Eve had power over it. If the mist moved up from the ground to water the earth, they had power over it. If the animals in the air and in the sea moved, they had power over them. If the trees moved in their growth and reproduction process, they had dominion over the trees and vegetation. If the waters in the seas, rivers, and streams moved on the earth, Adam and Eve had power over it.

God gave them power and dominion over *everything and all* things that moved on the earth. Adam and Eve were the delegated rulers of the earth. God had delegated the authority to them.

AUTHORITY TO RULE

"But of the tree of the knowledge of good and evil and blessing and calamity you shall not eat, for in the day that you eat of it you shall surely die."
(Genesis 2:17)

Although Adam and Eve enjoyed a life of ruler-ship and dominion, this life would and did not go uncontested, nor will our authority in Jesus Christ go uncontested. Elohim had given them instructions regarding the *limitation* of their authority. Adonai, Elohim's government had been established for the earth and everything that He created which lived on the earth.

The moral law had been established as well as the judicial laws, which governed the authority of every creature in the heavens and earth. As the creator and Lord, Elohim in His wisdom, set the order, the authority, and the position, of every creature. Thus, Elohim empowered Adam and Eve with several types of authority to govern the earth.

For example, numerous types of authority were delegated to Adam and Eve such as: the authority to bear the image and likeness of the Almighty. They had authority to reproduce their kind (be fruitful and multiply).

They had authority to make decisions and the authority to rule over the earth. They also had military authority to enforce the rules and government on the earth.

In addition, they had authority to make decisions regarding the care of the earth, which included the authority to choose to eat of the tree of knowledge of good and evil. Finally they had the authority to relinquish their delegated authority to someone or something else.

In addition to giving authority to Adam and Eve, Elohim set up a level of authority in His kingdom. See the diagram below.

Genesis 1:1 Before the creation of Man	Psalm 8:5 After Creation of Man
1. God-Elohim 2. Archangels 3. Angels	1. God-Elohim 2. Adam & Eve (humans) 3. Archangels (including Lucifer) 4. Angels

"For thou hast made him but little lower than God, And crownest him with glory and honor. (Psalm 8:5)

Man was created in the image and likeness of God. There is no other creature mentioned in the Bible, which bears the image and likeness of The Almighty. Moreover, no other creature is given the authority to rule over Elohim's creation other than man. God elevated man to this position according His sovereign will.

Man is the only creature that can reproduce offspring, which bear the image and likeness of Elohim. As I stated above, this authority delegated to man, did not go uncontested. God's archenemy, Satan, not only contested this authority but also cunningly stole this authority from Adam and Eve.

STOLEN AUTHORITY

"A man's (moral) self shall be filled with the fruit of his mouth; and with the consequence of his words he must be satisfied (whether good or evil). Death and life are in the power of the tongue, and

they who indulge in it shall eat the fruit of it (for death or life)" (Proverb 18:20-21) (Matt. 12:37)

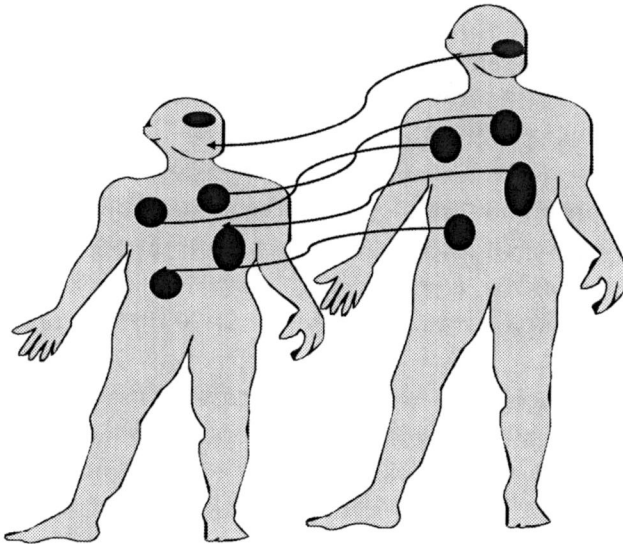

This illustrates how Satan infected man with his attributes and character. Also shown is how Satan can attach himself to man using what he infected man with, such as the iniquity or unbelief. He had placed triggers in the man so that he could trigger certain emotions or behaviors in him.

Elohim's archenemy, Satan had tried to exalt himself above the throne of God and make himself like the Most High. (Isaiah 14) Satan's plan failed miserably causing him and his cohorts, whom he had deceived and tricked into following him, to be kicked out of heaven and reduced to enemies of God and all of God's creation.

Satan allowed iniquity and guilt to be found in him, which produced rebellion, treason, and disobedience, within him. This perversion perverted man from a blameless heart, to a heart filled with pride and haughtiness, earning him his eviction papers.

Satan lost his authority as the chief musician of God and became the chief adversary of God. Satan was cast out as a profane creature, from the mountain of God, and the guardian cherub drove him out from the midst of the stones of fire. (Ezekiel 28)

As a result of his eviction and disgrace, Satan became the chief outlaw and trafficker of perversion, violence, iniquity, guilt, pride, and death. Satan's sole aim was and is to usurp God's authority. Defeated and powerless to seize God's authority, Satan set out to set up his authority on earth.

"The thief comes only in order to steal and kill and destroy. I came that they may have and enjoy life, and have it in abundance (to the full, till it overflows." (John 10:10)

Once again, Satan set out to set up a kingdom for himself. His mission and sole aim is to steal, kill, and destroy. His prime target was man, God's most precious creation. Satan knew that he could not approach Adam and Eve as the author of perversion and iniquity. He had to disguise himself as an angel of light. So off to the Garden of Eden he goes, masquerading as an angel of illumination, concealing his true nature, as a trafficker of sin and death.

Not only did Satan carry within himself violence and death, he also carried within himself timidity, cowardice, and the fear of death. God gave Adam and Eve authority over Satan and all his cohorts. The sprit of timidity and the spirit of cowardice were used to blind Eve (disguised) as gentle as a dove, thereby allowing Satan to entice and seduce her into disobeying God.

PRAYER:

Father God, I thank you for opening my understanding through the power of Your Holy Spirit. I ask that you reveal to me what my authority is as Your child heir and joint-heir with Jesus. I ask for Your enabling power to walk in the authority that you have provided for me through my union with Your Son, Jesus. Father, empower me to recognize the angel of light when he tries to deceive me. I plead the Blood of Jesus over my spirit, soul, and body, to shield me from all deception from the angel of light and all his cohorts. I bring the Blood of Jesus Christ to bear on all the works of the enemy to prevent me from walking in the faith, courage, and the truth, which God provides. I thank You Father, for the finished work of the cross, applied to my life in Jesus' name. Amen. So be it.

CHAPTER TEN

EXAMPLES OF TIMIDITY AND COWARDICE PART I

⌒≈⌒

"He said, I heard the sound of You (walking) in the garden, and I was afraid because I was naked; and I hid myself. And He said, Who told you that you were naked? Have you eaten of the tree of which I commanded you that you should not eat? And the man said, The woman whom You gave to be with me—she gave me (fruit) from the tree, and I ate. And the Lord God said to the woman, What is this you have done? And the woman said, The serpent beguiled (cheated, outwitted, and deceived) me, and I ate. (Genesis 3:10-13)

HIDING AND SHIFITING RESPONSIBILITY

Once Satan got his hooks into Adam and Eve he could pull their chains (See illustration on page 15, 19, & 61). The first thing Adam did when he heard God coming to meet with him was to hide. Why did Adam and Eve hide themselves? It was because Satan had flooded their hearts with darkness and darkness always flees from light. Satan had imparted timidity and cowardice into their hearts.

The second thing Adam did when God called out to him was to respond in timidity and cowardice. *"He said, I heard the sound of You (walking) in the garden, and I was afraid because I was naked; and I hid myself."* What was once reverential awe of God had now become perverted timidity and cowardice.

Thirdly, both Adam and Eve started shifting blame and slandering one another to God. For example, Adam blamed God for giving him his wife, Eve. It was God's fault (what had happen was not his fault). Then Adam accused God for setting him up. If God had not given him a wife, he would never have eaten the fruit. Eve followed Adam's lead by blaming the serpent and then accusing the serpent of tricking her.

What a picture of us today. It is like looking in the mirror. We do something we know that is wrong and when we get caught we blame someone else. We do not arrive at church on time so we blame our children for not getting dressed on time. Who's responsible for our children? As parents, we are.

Who has the authority in a family? The parents! Who should we blame for not arriving at church on time? The persons God has given the responsibility and the authority too, The Parents!

CONSEQUENCE

Both Adam and Eve lost their right to rule over creation. They severed their intimate relationship with God and subjected themselves to Satan. They became children of disobedience ruled by the prince of the power of the air, of the spirit that is now working in the sons of disobedience (Ephesians 2:2).

LYING - ABRAM CALLING HIS WIFE SISTER

"And when he was about to enter into Egypt, he said to Sarai his wife, I know that you are beautiful to behold. So when the Egyptians see you, they will say, This is his wife; and they will kill me, but they will let you live. Say, I beg of you, that you are my sister, so that it may go well with me for your sake and my life will be spared because of you.
(Genesis 12:1-13)

For fear of his life, Abram lied to the Egyptian King about Sarai. Abram's timidity towards death and his lack of trust in the Lord to protect him from the Egyptians, led him to lie and to get Sarai to lie. Some would argue that Sarai was Abram half-sister, but this is not the point. Abram's fabrication was Sarai was not his wife. Pharaoh's officials took Sarai into Pharaoh's house because Abram did not tell them that Sarai was his wife.

CONSEQUENCE

Pharaoh paid Abram for Sarai thinking that Sarai was Abram's sister. God struck Pharaoh and his entire household with a plague for Pharaoh having taken Sarai as part of his concubine. Pharaoh had Abram and all Abram's household escorted out of his country. It would appear that Abram escaped God's judgment for lying. On the contrary, Abram's sin found him out (Numbers 32:23) and caused him to be banished from Egypt.

Abram's sin became a generational sin. His son Isaac committed the same sin. In addition, two generations later, Abram's great grandson was sold into Egypt, imprisoned, and his descendents were kept in slavery for four hundred years.

In Exodus 34:7, God said that, *"Keeping mercy and loving-kindness for thousands, forgiving iniquity and transgression and sin, but Who will by no means clear the guilty, visiting the iniquity of the fathers upon the children and the children's children, to the third and fourth generation."* God restates this in Numbers 14:18 and again in Deuteronomy 5:9. God ranks lying in the category of idolatry. (See Revelation 21:8)

FLEEING - JACOB FLEEING FROM LABAN

"Jacob answered Laban, because I was afraid; for I thought, suppose you would take your daughters from me by force." (Genesis 31:31)

God had kept the covenant that He made with Jacob (Genesis 28:11-22). While living with Laban, everything that Jacob put his hands to, flourished, yet Jacob allowed Laban to intimidate him, succumbing to timidity and cowardice, to the point were he fled by night.

When Laban caught up with Jacob, Jacob admitted his fearfulness. Timidity and cowardice will make a person hide and seek escape by night. The person will withdraw and take the way of lest resistance, whether the way of lest resistance is godly or ungodly.

CONSEQUENCE

Jacob had to move his family in a frenzy in the night. In fear, Rachel took Laban's household idol to protect them on their journey. God had proven that He was with Jacob by prospering him. Rachel also lied to both Jacob and Laban regarding the idol.

Jacob's departure under the cover of night, could have given those people surrounding him, the impression that

Jacob's God was not faithful to him and was unable to protect him from his enemies. Likewise, we should be cognizant of the messages that we send out to others by our conduct. Our conduct always sends a message about our God, whether good or bad or true or false.

COWARDLY SUBMISSIVE

"And Moses said to Aaron, What did this people do to you, that you have brought so great a sin upon them? And Aaron said, Let not the anger of my lord blaze hot; you know the people that they are set on evil. For they said to me, Make us gods which shall go before us; as for this Moses, the man who brought us up out of the land of Egypt, we do not know what has become of him. I said to them, Those who have any gold, let them take it off. So they gave it to me; then I cast it into the fire, and there came out this calf. And when Moses saw that the people were unruly and unrestrained (for Aaron had let them get out of control, so that they were a derision and object of shame among their enemies)" *(Exodus 32:21-25)*

To me, this is one of the saddest events in the Bible. God had delivered His people from the bondage of the Egyptians. He started building Israel into a Nation-Army and by the breath of His mouth; He gave them His instructions (commandments) to Moses, to give to this Nation-Army.

God had given the Israelites the wealth of the Egyptians, parted the Red Sea, destroyed the entire Egyptian army, provided them water in the desert, and rained manna from heaven. Glory! What a Mighty God, what a mighty demonstration of His power and faithfulness. We would think that this was enough to keep the Israelites faithful to God, on the contrary.

Aaron was the spokesman for pronouncing the many plagues against the Egyptians. God made Aaron equal to Pharaoh, the king of the whole world at that time. Aaron would be what we call today, "the man with the power", but Aaron did not use his power, nor his authority, when he was put under pressure.

Aaron relinquished his authority and submitted to the whelm of the murmuring, grumbling, complaining, and rebellious people. Moses asked Aaron, "What did the people do to you that he had brought so great a sin upon them." (Exodus 32:21) Aaron allowed timidity to come in and then the spirit of cowardice. Timid behavior will lead to cowardice because timidity is cowardice's forerunner and scout.

Aaron had the authority God had given him. He could have called on God to intervene but he did not. What prevented Aaron from asking God to intervene? The answer is because timidity and cowardice paralyzed his mind so that he could not make sound decisions. Moses told Aaron that he, Aaron, had brought the sin upon the people. Moses told Aaron that because he was the one God had left in charge; he was responsible for what happened.

In like manner, when we relinquish the authority that God has delegated to us, we are the cause of whatever sin that is committed which could have been averted if we would have exercised our authority in Christ Jesus. For example, a pastor would not allow a want-a-be praise leader, who does not come to prayer meetings, does not show up to service on time, and has zero anointing as a praise leader, to lead praise and worship just because she is the only person that plays the piano.

The congregation wants music for the worship service; however, the pastor cannot connect (in the spirit) with this person and does not have the approval of God, to allow this person to lead praise and worship. However, if he submits to the complaining of his congregation, the anointing will lift from the pastor when she plays and his message is like lead to the congregation.

The congregation now thinks that the pastor is the problem (which he is) that is causing the problem and now wants to look for another pastor. This is a great sin. The pastor submitted (cowardly) to his congregation just as Aaron did in making the golden calf. What is your golden calf?

CONSEQUENCE

There is a great penalty for relinquishing our God given authority to ungodly demands as seen in the event with Aaron and the Israelites. Some three thousand Israelites died as a result of Aaron's sin. The vision and mission God gave the pastor has been aborted and the pastor has lost the anointing to minister the Word of God. Also the demands of the congregation were ungodly demands. Many ministers and ministries are destroyed by cowardice.

May God have mercy on all of us for the souls that die and go to hell because we have relinquished their authority God gave us to set them (captives) free from the bondage of Satan.

TREASON

"But the people who dwell there are strong, and the cities are fortified and very large; moreover, there we saw the sons of Anak (of great stature and courage). Amalek dwells in the land of the South (the Negeb); the Hittite, the Jebusite, and the Amorite dwell in the hill country; and the Canaanite dwells by the sea and along by the side of the Jordan (River). Caleb quieted the people before

Moses, and said, Let us go up at once and possess it; we are well able to conquer it. But his fellow scouts said, We are not able to go up against the people (of Canaan), for they are stronger than we are." (Numbers 13:28-31)

Treason is defined as surrender, a violation of allegiance toward one's country or sovereignty, especially the betrayal of one's own country by waging war against it or by consciously and purposely acting to aid its enemies. It also means betrayal of confidence or trust. (Webster's II New Riverside University Dictionary)

The Scouts that Moses sent out to scout out the land God promised to the Israelites, committed treason in two ways. One way was they subverted the people with their evil report, which turned the congregation of Israel against God and Moses. Moses was God's appointed leader. The second was they challenged their sovereign authority, God, and His honesty, regarding the conquest of the land.

Their focus on their own strength and the strength of the sons Anak, resulted in them seeing themselves as grasshoppers. This self-centeredness led them to rebel against God and subvert the whole nation.

Currently many of God's people subvert the appointed leaders of God because of their self-centeredness. For instance, God sends certain Christians to a specific ministry to aid the leadership in the vision that He has given the Pastor and that specific congregation.

These Christians know that God has sent them to the fellowship, however, because of their own self-centered agenda; they cannot see the vision of this ministry. They can only see a giant that they cannot conquer. In their minds, the giant is the Pastor who will not submit to their self-centered and selfish agenda. They resist the Pastor and subvert the congregation by under-minding the Pastor by complaining, showing up late for service, and projecting a negative attitude toward the Pastor.

In all cases cowardice eventually leads to treason in some form, weather through subversive and rebellious speech or outright physical acts.

> *"And all the congregation cried out with a loud voice, and (they) wept that night. All the Israelites grumbled and deplored their situation, accusing Moses and Aaron, to whom the whole congregation said, Would that we had died in Egypt! Or that we had died in this wilderness! Why does the Lord bring us to this land to fall by the sword? Our wives and little ones will be a prey. Is it not better for us to return to Egypt? (Acts 7:37-39.) And they said one to another, Let us choose a captain and return to Egypt. Then Moses and Aaron fell on their faces before all the assembly of Israelites."*
>
> *(Numbers 14:1-5)*

Grumbling and murmuring unchecked, as seen in the incident with the scouts, leads to murder if God does not intervene. The scout's timid and cowardly behavior infected the entire nation with slander against God and his appointed leader. Rebellion and treason followed. Unbelief under girds (supports, or strengthens) timidity and cowardice and these three always lead to treason against God and His plans.

CONSEQUENCE

The people attempted to stone Caleb and Joshua because Caleb and Joshua wanted to protect Moses and Aaron. The people rebelled against God and accused God of bringing them into the desert to murderer them and their children. As a result the people's unbelief and treasonous behavior, God ordered them into the wilderness until the entire generation died in the wilderness.

Consequently, Joshua, Caleb, and their family members where the only people from their generation to enter the promise land that God had promised them.

CHAPTER ELEVEN

EXAMPLE OF TIMIDITY AND COWARDICE PART II

"So about three thousand Israelites went up there, but they fled before the men of Ai."

(Joshua 7:4)

A THIEF AND LOSS OF BATTLES

The Israelites went to fight against the men of Ai. Because of the sin committed by Achan they were routed like whimpering cowards. Achan had stolen things God had devoted to destruction when they conquered Jericho. Timidity and cowardice will lead people to steal. Achan hid the things devoted for destruction in his tent (hiding something is characteristic of timidity and cowardice).

A thief is a person that is too timid to accept the place that God has ordained for his life at that present time. He wants more than what God is willing to give him. He is too timid to pray until God will give it to him and too cowardly to be content with what he has.

A covet hearted person will covertly or overtly take something that does not belong them. For example, a person that has been hired for an administrative job, whether at church or at some secular organization, and that person wants to be the manager of the section that she or he has been hired for. However, He or she does not qualify for the manager's position.

This person begins to under-mind the manager because he or she covets their job. Not only does he or she under-mind the manager, but he or she begins to subtly slander the manager to the manager's supervisor. When these tactics do not work, he or she will then start complaining, that they are being mistreated by the manager. The problem is covetedness. This person is too timid and cowardly to go out and obtain the stills needed to be a manager. They resort to taking something that does not belong to them.

CONSEQUENCE

The Israelites lost the battle with Ai. Achan, his family, and all his property were burned. God will judge us for submitting to the spirit of timidity and the sprit of cowardice. It is in our power to be free from the evil one. Soldiers of the Cross, we must resist the enemy in every point and area of our lives. Jesus has given us victory.

FAIL TO DESTROY OUR GOLIATH

"And all the men of Israel, when they saw the man, fled from him, terrified. And the Israelites said, Have you seen this man who has come out? Surely he has come out to defy Israel; and the man who kills him the king will enrich with great riches, and will give him his daughter and make his father's house free (from taxes and service) in Israel. And

David said to the men standing by him, What shall be done for the man who kills this Philistine and takes away the reproach from Israel? For who is this uncircumcised Philistine that he should defy the armies of the living God?"

(I Samuel 17:24-26)

Every soldier of the Cross, will have a Goliath that threatens and challenges his or her faith. Your Goliath may be that you are overweight and compulsive spending. It may be slanderer, procrastination, or unfaithfulness to God, or a commitment that you made with someone. It could be dishonesty or unbelief.

Our Goliath can be our job, money, or some type of sexual bondage. Satan is using these Goliaths to accuse us day and night before God. He is sending reinforcement to keep these Goliaths operating in our lives. Dear soldier of the Cross, do not let timidity and cowardice keep you in bondage to this Goliath.

Do not hide in foxholes and trenches and allow this uncircumcised Philistine to defile the ranks of God's army. Do not do like the Israelites did who stayed in their foxholes and trenches hiding and waiting for someone who would go out and fight the giant for them.

Do not get angry with those who fight their Goliath but rather join them. Take courage and run into the battle as David did in the name of Jesus and smite these enemies. Timidity will fall to its knees under the power of the precious blood of Jesus. The sword of the Spirit will cut off the head of Goliath. In the name of Jesus is victory.

CONSEQUENCE

Failing to defeat our Goliath keeps us hid in the foxholes and trenches. We are left immobile. We cannot move and be effective for God. Our conduct (hiding) gives the enemy the right to make all kinds of accusation against us before God.

Accusations such as, they don't believe in Jehovah! Look at them they have all that power Jesus gave them and they are hiding in their foxholes and trenches. Beloved, gird yourself with the courage of God, because in His courage we are assured victory.

INSUBORDERNATION AGAINST GOD

"When the men of Israel saw that they were in a tight situation—for their troops were hard pressed—they hid in caves, holes, rocks, tombs, and pits or cisterns. Some Hebrews had gone over the Jordan to the land of Gad and Gilead. As for Saul, he was still in Gilgal, and all the people followed him trembling. Saul waited seven days, according to the set time Samuel had appointed. But Samuel had not come to Gilgal, and the people were scattering from Saul. So Saul said, Bring me the burnt offering and the peace offerings. And he offered the burnt offering (which he was forbidden to do). And just as he finished offering the burnt offering, behold. Samuel came! Saul went out to meet and greet him. Samuel said, What have you done? Saul said. Because I saw that the people were scattering from me, and that you did not come within the days appointed, and that the Philistines were assembled at Michmash. I thought, the Philistines will come down now upon me to Gilgal, and I have not made supplication to the Lord. So I forced myself to offer a burnt offering. And Samuel said to Saul. You have done foolishly! You have not kept the commandment of the Lord you God which He commanded you; for the Lord would have established your kingdom over

**Israel forever; But now your kingdom shall not
continue; the Lord has sought out (David) a man
after His own heart, and the Lord has commanded
him to be prince and ruler over His people, because
you have not kept what the Lord commanded you."
(I Samuel 13:6-14)**

According to God's law, only the priest could offer a
sacrifice. Any act outside of God's expressed will is insubordination and every action of insubordination results in a
loss of authority. This may be a temporary loss, but it will
still be a lost.

CONSEQUENCE

Saul lost his kingdom and his inheritance. We lose our
position of authority and inheritance when we disobey God.
For example, Jesus promised us that we would do greater
works than He did. We are acting insubordinately when
we allow unbelief to hinder us from doing what Jesus has
commanded us to do.

ALLOW A USURPER TO TAKE A GOD GIVEN POSITION

*"And there came a messenger to David, saying,
The hearts of the men of Israel have gone after
Absalom. David said to all his servants who were
with him at Jerusalem, Arise and let us flee, or else
none of us will escape from Absalom. Make haste
to depart, lest he overtake us suddenly and bring
evil upon us and smite the city with the sword. And
the king's servants said to the king, Behold, your
servants are ready to do whatever my lord the king
says. So the king and all his household after him*

went forth. But he left ten women who were concu-
bines to keep the house."
(2 Sam. 12:11; 20:3.) (2 Samuel 15:13-16)

Absalom had murdered his brother, Amnon for raping his sister Tamar, David's daughter. According to the law, Absalom was to be put to death (Leviticus 24:17). As king over Israel, David did not have the right to pardon Absalom. This was a tragic thing to happen to a father. First his daughter is rapped by her brother, the king's son. Secondly, his son is murdered by his brother, the king's son.

Yes, this was a horrible thing for a father, yet this father was no ordinary father, this father was God's anointed king over Israel. This king-father had the responsibility of enforcing the laws of God, in accordance with the laws given by Moses.

Consequently, David's failure to administer justice and enforce the law resulted in Absalom rebelling against him to overthrow him as king over Israel. Was David a coward? Was David a timid man? When it came to battles with foreign enemies David was superior in battle.

On the battlefield David was a Goliath killer. Was David afraid of Absalom? Surely not, however, David was timid in making decisions regarding his personal life, just as we have different areas in our life were we are bold and strong in one area and timid and cowardly in another area.

As the king of Israel, David should have ordered Absalom to be put to death. It was David's duty to put down all insurrections against the nation. God requires His leaders to make difficult decisions when he puts them in positions of authority.

CONSEQUENCE

David had to flee and leave ten women in charge of the palace. He failed to destroy his Goliath. If we do not overcome our Goliaths they will overcome us. David's timid response to Absalom, regarding the murder of Absalom's brother, released murder and rebellion, that plagued David's descendants for generations.

LIVE AS UNDERCOVER CHRISTIANS TO AVOID PERSECUTION

"NOW THERE was a certain man among the Pharisees named Nicodemus, a ruler (a leader, an authority) among the Jews, Who came to Jesus at night and said to Him, Rabbi, we know and are certain that You have come from God (as) a Teacher; for no one can do these signs (these wonderworks, these miracles—and produce the proofs) that You do unless God is with him." (John 3:1-2)

Social pressures, peer pressure, and religious status, caused Nicodemus to come to Jesus by night. Nicodemus was a ruler of God's people, yet he was afraid to be seen in public with Jesus. Nicodemus knew that Jesus was not popular with some of the high-ranking Jewish officials. He knew that being seen with Jesus could put him on the "rejection" and "shunning" list. Persecution from the in-crowd was eminent when someone associated with someone in the "outcast- crowd".

Some faint-heart Christians are what we call under-cover Christians. They go underground on their jobs, in their social circles outside the walls of the church building.

When they are with other under-cover Christians they are loud and boastful, yet as soon as someone from the world in-crowd comes in they get quiet and try to sneak out unnoticed. I'm sure you have met a few haven't you. Do not get angry with them Beloved, pray that God would give them courage to serve Him in spirit and truth at all times.

> *"His parents said this because they feared (the leaders of) the Jews; for the Jews had already agreed that if anyone should acknowledge Jesus to be the Christ, he should be expelled and excluded from the synagogue."*
>
> *(John 9:22)*

The parents of the young man, who Jesus cured of blindness, buckled under the spirit of timidity and the sprit of cowardice, when the leaders of the synagogue asked them about their son. When pressure comes to us, the spirit of timidity and the spirit of cowardice are crouched at our door waiting to get in. WE must bolt our doors with the blood of Jesus to keep these destroyers out.

CONSEQUENCE

Timidity and cowardice influenced the parents of the young man who was cured of his blindness to lie to the religious leaders. Wherever these two spirits are, a lying spirit will accompany them. God requires His people to speak truth.

DENY THE LORD

> *"Now Peter was sitting outside in the courtyard, and one maid came up to him and said, You were also with Jesus the Galilean! But he denied it falsely before them all, saying, I do not know what you mean. And when he had gone out to*

the porch, another maid saw him, and she said to the bystanders, This fellow was with Jesus the Nazarene! And again he denied it and disowned Him with an oath, saying, I do not know the Man! After a little while, the bystanders came up and said to Peter, You certainly are one of them too, for even your accent betrays you. Then Peter began to invoke a curse on himself and to swear, I do not even know the Man! And at that moment a rooster crowed. (Matthew 26:69-74)

To the pure (in heart and conscience) all things are pure, but to the defiled and corrupt and unbelieving nothing is pure; their very minds and consciences are defiled and polluted. They profess to know God (to recognize, perceive, and be acquainted with Him), but deny and disown and renounce Him by what they do; they are detestable and loathsome, unbelieving and disobedient and disloyal and rebellious, and (they are) unfit and worthless for good work (deed or enterprise) of any kind." (Titus 1:15-16)

We've all heard the story of Peter and his denial of Jesus on the night that Jesus was betrayed by Judas and taken before the Sanhedrin in a mock-trail. But few of us are aware of how we deny Jesus in our daily conduct.

In Titus 1:16, Paul shows us how we can profess to know Jesus, but deny, disown, and renounce, Jesus by our conduct. If we constantly disobey Jesus, constantly walk in unbelief, and are constantly disloyal to Jesus, we are denying Jesus by our daily conduct.

Peter was faced with a life-threatening situation. But in our daily lives we are not, at least, most of us are not. Yet we allow intimidating, godly people keep us from standing up for Jesus. For example, a "starter-Christian." A starter-

Christian is similar to the fans of a football team, they wear a jacket with the team name on it but they are not part of the team.

CONSEQUENCE

> *"They profess to know God (to recognize, perceive, and be acquainted with Him), but deny and disown and renounce Him by what they do; they are detestable and loathsome, unbelieving and disobedient and disloyal and rebellious, and (they are) unfit and worthless for good work (deed or enterprise) of any kind." (Titus 1:16)*

Playing with God is a dangerous thing. A person that says they belong to God and then deny Him in their conduct is detestable before God.

CHAPTER TWELVE

GOD'S COMMANDS REGARDING TIMIDITY AND COWARDICE

"And Moses called to Joshua and said to him in the sight of all Israel, Be strong, courageous, and firm, for you shall go with this people into the land which the Lord has sworn to their fathers to give them, and you shall cause them to possess it. It is the Lord Who goes before you; He will (march) with you; He will not fail you or let you go or forsake you; (let there be no Cowardice or Flinching, but) fear not, neither become broken (in spirit—depressed, dismayed, and unnerved with alarm." (Deuteronomy 31:7-8 emphasis mine)

Moses and Joshua's lives are examples for God's people to emulate. Both Moses and Joshua are also types of Jesus Christ. These men of God had the same weaknesses as we do. They were not exempt from the dangers and toils of life. They had families that needed their care. The missions God commissioned them to do far exceed their human ability.

Yes, they were subject to every possible attack from the devil as we are. Yet, God *commanded* them not to let any cowardice or flinching be found in them. These men of God were prohibited from becoming timid and cowardly or flinching. In addition, they could not become broken, depressed in spirit, dismayed, or unnerved with alarm. God is not telling His men and women of war not to express emotions; however He is telling them that they must be able to distinguish between godly human emotions and spirits sent from Satan to afflict their spirit, soul, and body.

Bear with me for a moment. Depression is one of the major illnesses that plagues a major percentage of the American population. It is believe that one in five Americans suffers from some form of depression. Christians are not exempt from depression. Yet, how can this be so for Christians when God command us not to be depressed, dismayed, (faint hearted) or unnerved with alarm?

In addition, Isaiah 61:3 God says that He will give His people the garment of praise for *the spirit of heaviness*. The word *heaviness* is the Hebrew word *kahah*, pronounced *kaw-haw, (3543)* which means to be weak, to despond, or to grow dull. It also means, to darken, be dim, to fail, to faint, and to restrain.

The spirit of heaviness does not originate from God. Depression and despondency is not from God. Faint-heartiness does not come from God. These emotions are sent from hell to torment God's people. Am I saying that all depression comes from Satan; no I am not. Depression in some cases is a result of some physical problems and requires physical treatment.

What I am saying is that, most emotional and psychological problems that Christians suffer from are attacks from the pits of hell. I believe if the person would recognize that this is a spiritual attack and it must be resisted, according to the Word of God that this oppression would lift from the person.

JESUS' STANTANCE ON TIMIDITY AND COWARDICE

"Also (Jesus) told them a parable to the effect that they ought always to pray and not to turn coward (faint, lose heart, and give up)."

(Luke 18:1)

Jesus commands and God's commands are the same. This is apparent by Jesus commanding His disciples not to turn coward, faint, lose heart, or give up.

We can deceive ourselves with any type of excuse to keep us from confronting this spirit in our lives, but this spirit will hound us, until it destroy us. If we refuse to confront it and defeat it in our lives, we will suffer severe consequences.

For instance Christians have accepted the worldview of "political correctness." To be politically correct, (PC) means that, a person or groups of people will alter their language and behavior to avoid offending another person or group of people. It also means conforming to a belief, a language or practice to prevent offending other groups of people, as in matters of belief, (religious) race, gender, sex, age, or sexual orientation.

Beloved, political correctness deals with our belief system. It puts constrains on words (language) that we use. It boxes us in and makes us *conform* to the worldview. Romans 12:2 tells us not to be conformed to this world or allow ourselves to be molded by the world.

For example, the worldview (political correct) teaches people to accept that there is nothing wrong with homosexual behavior. That there is nothing wrong with having sexual deviants as leaders of the church and that there is nothing wrong with homosexuals functioning in leadership positions in the church. God requires us to be Biblically correct (see Romans chapter 1).

Another example of political correctness (worldview) is to isolate oneself from someone who is being attacked by the "world in-group" so that you do not become a part of the "world outcast- group." Christians fall into this trap on their jobs and in certain social arenas.

For instant, when a Christian refuse to do something unethical on their job when directed by the "in-group." When that Christian refuses, that Christian becomes the enemy of the "world in-group." Instead of the other Christians in the work place rallying to their brother or sister in Christ, they stay aloof from them to avoid the persecution of being put into the "world outcast-group".

Again, the worldview (political correct) says that you must conform to ungodly beliefs (and a sometime behavior) as not to offend anyone. God requires us to be spiritually and morally correct (reference the whole Bible). The Bible says that,

> *"Great peace have they who love Your law: nothing shall offend them or make them stumble." (Psalm 119:165) "And in the same way the ones sown upon stony ground are those who, when they hear the Word, at once receive and accept and welcome it with you; And they have not real root in themselves, and so they endure for a little while; then when trouble or persecution arises on account of the Word, they immediately are offended (become displeased, indignant, resentful) and they stumble and fall away." (Mark 4:16-17)*

The word *offend* in the Hebrew is **mikshowl** (4383) which means, stumbling block, obstacle, enticement, (specifically to idols, (demon)), to cause to fall. It also means offense or ruin. The Greek word for *offend* is the word **skandalzo** (skan-dal-id'-z') (4624) and it means to entrap, to trip up, to scandalize, to entice to sin, apostasy, or displeasure.

Saints of God, you cannot take on the worldview and live upright before God. The Christian's weapons against offense are God's love and being rooted in His Word. Obviously, non-Christians are easily offended or quick to take offense because the love of God is not in their hearts. Their hearts and mind are darkened and the Word of God (in us) is an offense to them.

> *"We preach Christ (the Messiah) crucified, (preaching which) to the Jews is a scandal and an offensive stumbling block (that springs a snare or trap), and to the Gentiles it is absurd and utterly unphilosophical nonsense."*
> *(I Corinthians 1:23)*

On the other hand when Christians are easily offended or quick to take offense they are not operating "under the law" of God, which is to love Him and His law. The devil has deceived most Christians into believing that they are no longer under the law (instructions) of God, of the Old Testament.

If we are not under the law (instructions) of God, what are we under? No we should not practice the law of God concerning the ritual sacrifices of the temple in the Old Testament, but we are obligated to obey the rest of God's Word. Jesus came to fulfill the law of God.

> *"Do not think that I have come to do away with or undo the Law or the Prophets; I have not come to do away with or undo but to complete and fulfill them." (Matthew 5:17)*

Moreover, Jesus or Paul did not come to destroy or undo the Law of love.

"Love endures long and is patient and kind; love never is envious nor boils over with jealousy, is not boastful or vainglorious, does not display itself haughtily. It is not conceited (arrogant and inflated with pride); it is not rude (unmannerly) and does not act unbecomingly. Love (God's love in us) does not insist on its own rights or its own way, for it is not self-seeking; it is not touchy or fretful or resentful; it takes no account of the evil done to it (it pays no attention to a suffered wrong). (I Corinthians 13:4-5) Love bears up under anything and everything that comes, is ever ready to believe the best of every person, its hopes are fadeless under all circumstances, and it endures everything (without weakening). Love never fails (never fades out or becomes obsolete or comes to an end)"
(1 Corinthians 13:7-8)

God is love. Everything regarding God and God's people is governed and operates by God's law of love. Therefore, sons and daughters of God, if we are not walking in the love that God has imputed and imparted to us in our heart through the power of the Holy Spirit, we must ask our selves the question God asked Adam and Eve after they disobeyed Him in the Garden of Eden. "Where are you? Where are you?"

By definition, being politically correct by the world system means, being controlled by idols, demons. The god of this world operates the world system. When we allow the world system of beliefs to control our lives, we are indirectly allowing Satan to control our lives.

This vile spirit of offense is the sons and the daughters of timidity and cowardice disguised under the cloak of political correctness. We can no longer let it control us, nor can ministries of God be timid and cowardly in dealing with ungodly behavior in the congregation of God, because they are fearful of offending the person professing to be a Christian, while living like those in the world.

Men and women of God are accountable to God for what they allow to go on in their lives and in the Body of Christ. We must confront the spirit of timidity and the spirit of cowardice regardless of what type of disguises they wear.

JESUS DID NOT LEAVE US A SPIRIT OF COWARDICE

"Peace I leave with you; My (own) peace I now give and bequeath to you. Not as the world gives do I give to you. Do not let your hearts be troubled, neither let them be afraid. (Stop allowing yourselves to be agitated and disturbed; and do not permit yourselves to be fearful and intimidated and cowardly and unsettled.)" (John 14:27)

Jesus bequeathed His peace to all His disciples. If we are disciples of Jesus Christ, we have Jesus' peace living in us. It is not like the temporal and fleeting peace the world gives. It is the eternal attribute of the Almighty God, imparted into your heart by the Lamb of God. Jesus' peace garrisons and builds a fortress around our heart so that fear, intimidation, cowardice, and unsettledness will not enter our hearts. (Philippians 4:7)

Consequently, Jesus commands His disciples not to permit themselves to become fearful, be intimidated, or become cowardly and unsettled. It is a command Beloved, not an option in the kingdom of God. We must resist all forms of intimidation, timidity, and cowardice. We cannot be fearful and easily unsettled by life circumstances.

For example, your company is downsizing and they have told you that you will probably loose your job. The Lord Jesus commands you not to be fearful, intimidated, timid, or cowardly and unsettled, regarding this matter. Jesus has commanded you to receive the peace He has bequeathed to you.

Moreover, the word *bequeath* is a legal term which means something has been conferred to someone or has been bestowed or handed down to someone as an inheritance. We have inherited Jesus peace. We are an heir and join-heir with Jesus Christ. Therefore we must obey God the Father, God the Son, and God the Holy Ghost, we must receive His peace.

THE MANDATE FOR GOD'S SOLDIERS

"For God did not give us a spirit of timidity (of cowardice, of craven and cringing and fawning fear), but (He has given us a spirit) of power and of love and of calm and well-balanced mind and discipline and self-control. Do not blush or be ashamed then, to testify to and for our Lord, nor of me, a prisoner for His sake, but (with me) take your share of the suffering (to which the preaching) of the Gospel (may expose you, and do it) in the power of God."
(2 Timothy 1:7-8)

It is evident that it is a mandate from God to His people to resist timidity and cowardice as enemies. God's people cannot allow timidity and cowardice to rule and govern their lives. We must rid ourselves of timidity whether it is cloaked in over-sensitivity or concealed in some form of weakness. We must learn to discern it and rid ourselves of it. Cowardice can masquerade itself as offense or guise itself as political correctness.

It can camouflage itself as depression and despondency and deceive a person into thinking that it is a normal response to some emotional or psychological trauma. Beloved there were no psychologist on Jesus ministry staff. Nor did David call in a psychologist when his son Amnon, rapped his daughter Tamar, nor when Absalom, killed his son Amnon, and subverted his authority as king over Israel. No, God sent His prophet to David and David turned his face to God saying,

"Fret not yourself because of evildoers, neither be envious against those who work unrighteousness (that which is not upright or in right standing with God). For they shall soon be cut down like the grass, and wither as the green herb. Trust (lean on, rely on, and be confident) in the Lord and do good; so shall you dwell in the land and feed surely on His faithfulness, and truly you shall be fed. Delight yourself also in the Lord, and He will give you the desires and secret petitions of your heart. Commit your way to the Lord (roll and repose each care of your load on Him); trust (lean on, rely on, and be confident) also in Him and He will bring it to pass. And He will make your uprightness and right standing with God go forth as the light, and your justice and right as (the shining sun of) the noonday. Be still and rest in the Lord; wait for Him and patiently lean yourself upon Him; fret not yourself because of him who prospers in his way, because of the man who brings wicked devices to pass. Cease from anger and forsake wrath; fret not yourself—it tends only to evildoing. For evildoers shall be cut off, but those who wait and hope and look for the Lord (in the end) shall inherit the earth."

(Isa 57:13) (Psalm 37:1-9)

Depression, despondency, timidity, and cowardice do not come to do us as something good. They come to do us evil. They are evildoers. They are Goliaths. Our God will cut them down like grass and they will wither away like the green herb.

Jehovah is the, All Sufficient One and He is the same yesterday, today and forever. What God did for David He will do for all of His people. Receive the blessing of the Lord and receive the peace that Jesus has conferred upon us.

CHAPTER THIRTEEN

OVERCOMING THE SPIRIT OF TIMIDITY AND COWARDICE PART I

⟨≈⟩

"AND YOU (He made alive), when you were dead (slain) by (your) trespasses and sins In which at one time you walked (habitually). You were following the course and fashion of this world (were under the sway of the tendency of this present age), following the prince of the power of the air. (You were obedient to and under the control of) the (demon) spirit that still constantly works in the sons of disobedience (the careless, the rebellious, and the unbelieving, who go against the purposes of God). Among these we as well as you once lived and conducted ourselves in the passions of our flesh (our behavior governed by our corrupt and sensual nature), obeying the impulses of the flesh and the thoughts of the mind (our cravings dictated by our senses and our dark imaginings). We were then by nature children of (God's) wrath and heirs of (His) indignation, like the rest of mankind. But God—so rich is He in His mercy! Because of and in order to satisfy the great and wonderful and

intense love with which He loved us, Even when we were dead (slain) by (our own) shortcomings and trespasses, He made us alive together in fellowship and in union with Christ; (He gave us the very life of Christ Himself, the same new life with which He quickened Him, for) it is by grace (His favor and mercy which you did not deserve) that you are saved (delivered from judgment and made partakers of Christ's salvation). And He raised us up together with Him and made us sit down together (giving us joint seating with Him) in the heavenly sphere (by virtue of our being) in Christ Jesus (the Messiah, the Anointed One)."(Eph 2:1-6)

I have identified this enemy. Now I will give ways to defeat theses enemies. These tools are not all inclusive. As you seek the Lord He will give you more insight.

Jesus Christ has redeemed us by His blood. By one man's sin (Adam) humanity was separated from God (spiritually dead) and by one man's righteousness all those who choose to accept Jesus Christ as their Lord and Savior has been delivered from the hands of Satan and all his works.

Jesus' finished work on the Cross, has delivered us who were dead in our trespasses and sins. Through the blood of Jesus we have become sons and daughters of obedience, we are no longer sons and daughters of disobedience, who are under the control of the (demon) spirits that still constantly work in the sons and daughters disobedience.

Soldiers of the Cross, we have miraculously been made alive, brought together in fellowship with Jesus Christ. We are now in union with Jesus Christ. Jesus has also raised us up together with Him and made us sit down together (giving us joint seating with Him) in the heavenly sphere as a result of us being in Jesus. (See illustration below).

MAN IN CHRIST

Man in Christ Jesus

Satan under Jesus feet

Satan

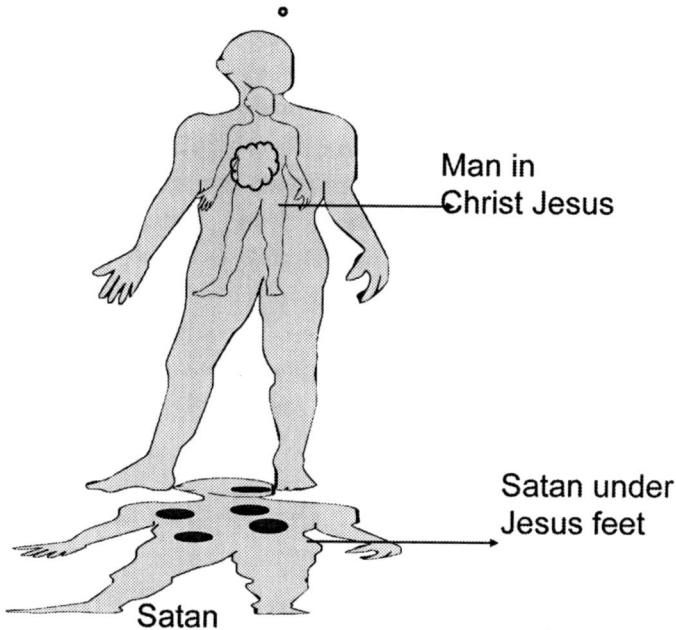

SATAN IS UNDER JESUS FEET

"Far above all rule and authority and power and dominion and every name that is named (above every title that can be conferred), not only in this age and in this world, but also in the age and the world which are to come." (Ephesians 1:21)

The illustration gives us an animated picture of how we are positioned in Christ Jesus. We are in Him. Being in Him places us in a position of authority. As He is, so are we. God has raised Him up and seated Him at His right hand. We are there with Christ.

God has put all things under the feet of Jesus. We are in Christ Jesus therefore all things are under our feet. In the name of Jesus, we have dominion and authority over all the powers of the enemy. We must appropriate the authority Jesus has given us. We do this by declaring and decreeing things that are not as though they were, in the name of Jesus.

For example, I decree that the blessings of God mentioned in Deuteronomy chapter 28, are mine according to the Word of God. I decree in the name of Jesus, these blessing that God has commanded toward me now, over me in the name of Jesus.

The spirit of timidity is under Jesus feet. The spirit of cowardice is under Jesus feet. The name timidity and the name cowardice must bow to the name of Jesus Christ. We are victorious in Jesus.

JESUS HAS DISARMED SATAN AND ALL HIS EMPS

"Having cancelled and blotted out and wiped away the handwriting of the note (bond) with its legal decrees and demands which was in force and stood against us (hostile to us). This (note with its regulations, decrees, and demands) He set aside and cleared completely out of our way by nailing it to (His) cross. (God) disarmed the principalities and powers that were ranged against us and made a bold display and public example of them, in triumphing over them in Him and in it (the cross)." *(Colossians 2:14-15)*

God has disarmed the principalities and powers that try to assail us. He made a bold display of them before all the heavens and all the cosmos. The whole creation in heaven, in the earth, and below the earth, witnessed Satan's defeat.

We must allow the Holy Spirit to reveal this into our spirits so that we can walk in our legal position of victor over all the powers of the enemy. Jesus is victor and we are in Him, consequently we are victors. We have victory over the spirit of timidity and the spirit of cowardice. These spirits have indeed been disarmed by Jesus Christ and they no longer have power over God's people.

In addition to allowing the Holy Spirit to reveal this to us, we must believe in our hearts and confess with our mouth that we are victors in Jesus Christ. The same principle of faith we used for salvation is the same principle of faith that we use to walk in our position of victory.

For instance we believe what the Word of God says about us. We must believe this in our hearts. We then confess with our mouth what we believe in our hearts. For example, I believe in my heart, according to Colossian 2:14-15 that, Jesus Christ, my Savior, disarmed all principalities and powers and made an open show of them. I confess with my mouth that I am in Jesus Christ, and in the name of Jesus, I have taken my place of victor and I will walk in that victory. Amen, so be it.

We must see our position in Christ. Please examine the chart below. This is our legal position in Christ Jesus. Live and walk in it through the blood of Jesus and by the power of the Holy Spirit. We defeat the spirit of timidity and the spirit of cowardice by knowing who we are in Christ Jesus. In Hosea 4:6, God says that, *"My people are destroyed for lack of knowledge..."*

After the Creation of Man Genesis 2	After the Fall of Man Genesis 3	After the Cross and Resurrection of Jesus
God-Elohim	God-Jehovah	God-El Shaddai
Adam & Eve (humans)	Archangels	Man
Archangels	Lucifer-Archangel	Archangels
Lucifer Archangel	Angels	Lucifer-Archangel
Angels	Man	Angels

"(The Father) has delivered and drawn us to Himself out of the control and the dominion of darkness and has transferred us into the kingdom of the Son of His love."

(Colossians 1:13)

We live in two worlds. We live seated in heaven in Christ Jesus. This is our legal spiritual position. We live there, as citizens of heaven. We live in this world but we are not of this world. We are not of this world. Once we were born-again by the Spirit of God we are transferred into the kingdom of the Son, of His love.

CHAPTER FOURTEEN

OVERCOMING THE SPIRIT OF TIMIDITY AND COWARDICE PART II

SONS AND DAUGHTERS OF GOD ARE FILLED WITH THE GODHEAD

"For in Him the whole fullness of Deity (the Godhead) continues to dwell in bodily form (giving complete expression of the divine nature). And you are in Him, made full and having come to fullness of life (in Christ you too are filled with the Godhead—Father, Son and Holy Spirit—and reach full spiritual stature). And He is the Head of all rule and authority (of every angelic principality and power)." (Colossians 2:9-10)

If we have been born-again according to John 3:3-5 and Romans 10:8-11, we are sons and daughters of the Most High God. Jesus is the fullness of the Godhead. Jesus Christ is the fullness of the Father, Son, and Holy Spirit. Jesus Christ has transferred us into His kingdom. Jesus Christ the fullness of the Godhead lives within our spirit. Halleluiah! Glory – Halleluiah!

Praise God, Jesus Christ is the head of all rulers and all powers. We are in Him, the head of all rule, and all power. Therefore, we defeat the spirit of timidity and the spirit of cowardice with the words of our testimony. Our testimony is what we are in Him. We are those He has given power over all their enemies. We appropriate this victory by confessing that we are in Him, Jesus Christ, and the Greater One lives in us. Halleluiah!

"Little children, you are of God (you belong to Him) and have (already) defeated and overcome them (the agents of the antichrist), because He Who lives in you is greater (mightier) than he who is in the world."

(I John 4:4)

Shout for the Greater One, Jesus Christ, lives in you. Shout for the Greater One, Jesus Christ, is mightier that the spirit of timidity. Shout for the, Greater One, Jesus Christ, is mightier than the spirit of cowardice. Shout for the, Greater One, Jesus Christ, has already defeated and overcome the agents of the antichrist. This means that Jesus has overcome Satan and all his agents.

The fire of the Holy Spirit is within the sons and daughters of God. We must believe with all our hearts and confess with our mouths, that the fullness of the Godhead is within us, because of the Living Christ living in us. We must pull down all imagination and reasoning that exalts itself against the Word of God.

> *"For though we walk (live) in the flesh, we are not carrying on our warfare according to the flesh and using mere human weapons. For the weapons of our warfare are not physical (weapons of the flesh and blood), but they are mighty before God for the overthrow and destruction of strongholds, (Inasmuch as we) refute arguments and theories and reasoning and every proud and lofty thing that set itself up against the (true) knowledge of God; and we lead every thought and purpose away captive into the obedience of Christ (the Messiah, the Anointed One)." (2 Corinthians 10:3-5)*

We pull down, overthrow, and destroy strongholds that set itself up against the truth of God in us. We do this by putting our faith into action. We repent of any sin in our lives, which give place to enemy strongholds. We receive the cleansing power of the blood of Jesus in accordance with 1 John 1:9. We plead the blood of Jesus against these strongholds.

For example, in the name of Jesus, I plead the blood of Jesus, against the spirit of timidity and the spirit of cowardice that is influencing or operating in my live. In the name of Jesus Christ, I bring to bear the finished work of the Cross of Calvary against the spirit of timidity and the sprit of cowardice.

I bind these spirits in chains and fetters of iron and I dislodge them from me, from my home, from my church, and from the atmosphere, where I live, in Jesus name. God I ask you in the name of Jesus, to bring the Holy Spirit and the Blood of Jesus to bear in every area of my life, where these spirits have been operating, in Jesus name. Amen, it is so.

If these spirits have plagued you for a long period of time they will try to come back, therefore you must plead, the blood of Jesus, over you and your environment daily. Ask other Holy Spirit filled Christians to pray for you and over you regarding the strongholds in your life. Jesus Christ is the victor and we are in Him, therefore we are victors over all our strongholds.

OVERCOME BY THE CLEANSING POWER OF THE BLOOD OF JESUS

"But if we (really) are living and walking in the Light, as He (Himself) is in the Light, we have (true, unbroken) fellowship with one another, and the blood of Jesus Christ His Son cleanses (removes) us from all sin and guilt (keeps us cleansed from sin in all its forms and manifestations). If we (freely) admit that we have sinned and confess our sins, He is faithful and just (true to His own nature and promises) and will forgive our sins (dismiss our lawlessness) and (continuously) cleanse us from all unrighteousness (everything not in conformity to His will in purpose, thought, and action)."

(1 John 1:7-9)

We are cleansed by the blood of Jesus when we walk in obedience to the Light. This Light is Jesus Christ. We must walk in compliance with the Word of God. In addition, we must have unbroken fellowship with God; we must walk in unbroken fellowship with one another.

God instructs us to forsake not the assembly. This means that we should be a part of a local congregation. Within that local congregation we should have unbroken fellowship with those in the fellowship. Fellowship within the local body is required and the local body must fellowship with other local bodies with in the community or city.

Obedience to God's Word invokes the cleansing power of the blood of Jesus. Obedience to God puts in motion a spiritual law. That spiritual law is the "Law of the blood." In Leviticus 17:11 God tells us that,

"For the life (the animal soul) is in the blood, and I have given it for you upon the altar to make atonement for your souls; for it is the blood that makes atonement, by reason of the life (which it represents)." (Rom. 3:24-26.) (Leviticus 17:11)

The blood of Jesus cleanses our soul. It assists in the renewal of the mind (Romans 12:1-2). It brings life out of death. It removes all sins and guilt from us and keeps us cleansed from sin in all its forms and all is manifestations. The Law of Obedience precedes the Law of the blood.

The Law of the blood will not operate apart from the Law of Obedience and the Law of the Spirit. *"For the law of the Spirit of life (which is) in Christ Jesus (the law of our new being) has freed me from the law of sin and of death." (Romans 8:2)*

The Law of the Spirit produces life whereas the law of sin produces death. The law of the Spirit and the Law of the blood work in unison. *"And there are three witnesses on the* earth: *the Spirit, the water, and the blood; and these three agree (are in unison; their testimony coincides). (I John 5:8)* Therefore, we must obey all three laws to receive cleansing from all sins and all the manifestations of sin.

The spirit of timidity and the spirit cowardice is like all other spirits from Satan. These Wicked and evil spirits are attracted to spiritual filth. Disobedience and sin is a breading ground for spiritual trash and filth. It is a magnet for Satan and his cohorts. We must get rid of the spiritual muck and spiritual trash generated by disobedience and the practice of sin.

You may ask, *what if someone has sinned against me?* For example, an older brother or father has molested his daughter or younger sister. This is a sin against the daughter or sister. The sister is seriously wounded, and responds to the pain and woundedness with resentment, bitterness, and hatred. Although, these are normal responses to this tragedy, if the sister does not forgive her abuser she enters into his sin, because she is linked and chained to him through unforgiveness. Unforgiveness is a magnet for tormentors.

> *"Then his master called him and said to him, You contemptible and wicked attendant! I forgave and cancelled all that (great) debt of yours because you begged me to. And should you not have had pity and mercy on your fellow attendant, as I had pity and mercy on you? And in wrath his master turned him over to the torturers (the jailers), till he should pay all that he owed. So also My heavenly Father will deal with everyone of you if you do not freely forgive your brother from your heart his offenses."* *(Matthew 18:32-35)*

The spirit of timidity and the spirit of cowardice are torturers who torment those who refuse to forgive. If we confess our sin Jesus Christ is faithful to *forgive* us of our sins and cleanse us from all unrighteousness. God has given us the overcoming power, of the cleansing blood of Jesus Christ. We appropriate this overcoming power through obedience, repentance, and forgiveness.

OVERCOME WITH THE BLOOD OF JESUS

"And they have overcome (conquered) him by means of the blood of the Lamb and by the utterance of their testimony, for they did not love and cling to life even when faced with death (holding their lives cheap till they had to die for their witnessing)." (Revelation 12:11)

First, we conquer our enemy by the blood of the Lamb. We appropriate the blood of Jesus by pleading the blood. For example, Father God, I ask your forgiveness for any and all sins in my life (state the specific sins). I plead the blood of Jesus, over me, my family, and I appropriate its protective power. I plead the blood against the works of the enemy in my life and in the lives of all my family members. I do this through the power of the Holy Spirit and in the name of Jesus.

We overcome by the words of our testimony. Our life is our testimony. We must live in obedience to God. We implement the words of our testimony by our confessions (what we say), proclamations (what we proclaim), and our decrees (what we decree, the word of God over our lives, which is unalterable).

When we make a decree by our words we issue an edict into the unseen world, decreeing to the invisible world, what the Word of God says about us. For instance, I decree in accordance with 1 John 1:7&9, that the power, of the blood of Jesus, cleanses me from all sins and all its manifestations.

I further decree, based on these Scriptures that, Jesus, not only forgives me, but I forgive all those who have sinned against me, through the cleansing power of the blood of Jesus. In Jesus' name, I seal this as a decree, in the heavens and in the earth. Amen, so be it.

CHAPTER FIFTEEN

OVERCOMING THE SPIRIT OF TIMIDITY AND COWARDICE PART III

⁓⧫⁓

"And God's peace (shall be yours, that tranquil state of a soul assured of its salvation through Christ, and so fearing nothing from God and being content with its earthly lot of whatever sort that is, that peace) which transcends all understanding shall garrison and mount guard over your hearts and minds in Christ Jesus." (Philippians 4:7)

GARRISON YOUR HEART WITH PEACE

Jehovah Shalom is one of the redemptive names of God. Shalom is the Hebrew word for *peace*. God's peace transcends all reasoning and understanding. His peace also garrisons our hearts and minds. A *garrison* is a fortified place of protections. In addition to garrisoning our hearts and minds, God's peace will mount guard over our hearts and minds.

How can the peace of God mount a guard over our hearts and minds?

First, the word, *mount* means to equip with guns or arms. It also means to secure firmly. Thus, the peace of God surrounds our hearts and minds with His armory and provides security and protection against the onslaught from the spirit of timidity and the spirit of cowardice and against all forms of onslaught of the enemy.

Consequently, we can appropriate God's peace by *accepting* His peace. For example, Father God, I accept Your peace conferred upon me, by Your Son, Jesus Christ. In the name of Jesus, I receive You as Jehovah Shalom. Amen

PUT ON THE GARMENT OF PRAISE (Isaiah 61:3)

"To grant (consolation and joy) to those who mourn in Zion—to give them an ornament (a garland or diadem) of beauty instead of ashes, the oil of joy instead of mourning, the garment (expressive) of praise instead of a heavy, burdened, and failing spirit—that they may be called oaks of righteousness (lofty, strong, and magnificent, distinguished for uprightness, justice, and right standing with God), the planting of the Lord, that He may be glorified." (Isaiah 61:3)

Our covenant with God gives us access to all the blessings of Abraham. The *garment of praise* is a blessing from God. We can, by faith, receive this garment of praise. For instance, in the name of Jesus, I receive the garment of praise, instead of a heavy, burdened, and failing spirit. I yield myself to the Holy Spirit, for the release of this garment in and through my spirit. In Jesus name. Amen.

HEDGE YOURSELF IN TO PROTECT YOURSELF FROM THE ENEMY

"Therefore, behold, I (the Lord God) will hedge up her way (even yours, O Israel) with thorns; and I will build a wall against her that she shall not find her paths. (Hosea 2:6) Have You not put a hedge about him and his house and all that he has, on every side? You have conferred prosperity and happiness upon him in the work of his hands, and his possessions have increased in the land."

(Job 1:10)

A *hedge* is barrier, which encloses something. God has provided a hedge of protection for His people. God had a barrier between Job and Satan. God has a barrier between Satan and all His people. God is no respecter of persons. He does not discriminate in His love for His children. We must acknowledge this hedge and thank God for the hedge of protection that He has provided for us.

In Hosea chapter 2:6, Hosea was having a problem with his wife. By the inspiration of the Holy Spirit, Hosea placed a spiritual hedge of thorns, around her so that she could not find her old paths. As God's children we have the authority to hedge ourselves in so that we will not go back down the path of timidity and cowardice. What hedges us in can also hedge things out.

For example, in the name of Jesus, I hedge myself in, so that I will not return to the path set for me by the spirit of timidity and the spirit of cowardice. This hedge protects me from the spirit of timidity and cowardice, in Jesus' name. Amen

WALK IN THE AUTHORITY JESUS HAS DELEGATED TO YOU

"Behold! I have given you authority and power to trample upon serpents and scorpions, and (physical and mental strength and ability) over all the power that the enemy (possesses); and nothing shall in any way harm you."

(Luke 10:19)

Jesus conferred authority upon us; however we must use the authority that He has provided. By faith, we must apply the Blood of Jesus to every situation in our lives. By faith, we must pull down all strongholds arrayed against us. By faith, we must gird ourselves with the name of Jesus. By faith, we must put on righteous and be conformed to the image of Jesus Christ. I am not saying that we can just believe and things happen. No our faith must have corresponding actions.

For instance, I believe that Jesus gave me authority over the spirit of timidity. My corresponding action would be reading the word and resisting the attack from the spirit of timidity. If I am too timid to confront someone, who is phoning me too gossip, I cannot take authority over this spirit. Should I take authority over this spirit that keeps me from obeying the Lord, regarding listening to gossip. I must, with corresponding actions stop listening to gossip.

BE FILLED WITH THE SPIRIT OF GOD

"And do not get drunk with wine, for that is debauchery; but ever be filled and stimulated with the (Holy) Spirit." (Prov. 23:20.) (Ephesians 5:18)

Jesus commands up to be filled with the Holy Spirit. The Holy Spirit empowers us to do what God commands us to do. The Holy Spirit also empowers us to war against the spirit of timidity and cowardice. We must yield to Him, so that He can do His work in us.

BUILD YOUR SELF UP

"But you, beloved, build yourselves up (founded) on your most holy faith (make progress, rise like an edifice higher and higher), praying in the Holy Spirit."

(Jude 1:20)

Before we can build ourselves up in the Holy Spirit we must be first filled with the Holy Spirit as mentioned in Ephesians 5:18. Praying in the spirit, is allowing the Holy Spirit, to pray in our spirit. (Romans 8:26) Praying in tongues as the Holy Sprit gives the utterance is praying in the Spirit.

Praying in the spirit also helps us to make spiritual progress in being conformed to the image of Jesus. He is our empowerment to be transformed into mature and productive saints.

KEEP YOURSELF IN THE LOVE OF GOD

"Guard and keep yourselves in the love of God; expect and patiently wait for the mercy of our Lord Jesus Christ (the Messiah)—(which will bring you) unto life eternal." (Jude 1:21)

Love is the foundation of all things in the life of a believer. Jesus came in the flesh to redeem humanity because God so loved the world. We are born-again because Jesus first loved us. All things of God work by love (God's) because God is love.

Jude warned the saints to guard and keep themselves in love. This warning is for all of God saints. We must guard and keep the love of God that is shed abroad in our hearts by the Holy Spirit (Romans 5:5).

Our faith will not work, nor the faith of God, that is in us if we do not allow the love of God, to be shed abroad in our hearts, by the Holy Spirit. Moreover, *"For (if we are) in Christ Jesus, neither circumcision nor uncircumcision counts for anything, but only **faith** activated and energized and expressed and **working** through **love**." (Galatians 5:6)* Faith works through God's law of love by the power of the Holy Spirit that is in us. We must yield to the Holy Spirit for this work of love to be manifested in our lives.

For example, Holy Spirit, I yield myself to you so that you can release the love of God, in my heart. Through faith and in the name of Jesus, I receive the manifestation, of the love of God, in my heart.

"Love endures long and is patient and kind; love never is envious nor boils over with jealousy, is not boastful or vainglorious, does not display itself haughtily. It is not conceited (arrogant and inflated with pride); it is not rude (unmannerly) and does not act unbecomingly. Love (God's love in us) does not insist on its own rights or its own way, for it is not self-seeking; it is not touchy or fretful or resentful; it takes no account of the evil done to it (it pays no attention to a suffered wrong). It does not rejoice at injustice and unrighteousness, but rejoices when right and truth prevail. Love bears up under anything and everything that comes, is ever ready to believe the best of every person, its hopes are fadeless under all circumstances, and it endures everything (without weakening). Love never fails (never fades out or becomes obsolete or comes to

an end). As for prophecy (the gift of interpreting the divine will and purpose), it will be fulfilled and pass away; as for tongues, they will be destroyed and cease; as for knowledge, it will pass away (it will lose its value and be superseded by truth)." (I Corinthians 13:4-8)

IN CLOSING...

Beloved, God is love and all things that He has provided for us, are obtained through faith, which is activated by love. *"For (if we are) in Christ Jesus, neither circumcision nor uncircumcision counts for anything, but only **faith** activated and energized and expressed and **working** through **love**. (Galatians 5:6)* This love is shed abroad in our hearts by the Holy Spirit. We should ask God daily for this love to be released in us.

We all respond to God in different ways because God has wonderfully created us with individual distinctions. These distinctions are His way of showing us how much He loves us. We are each special, designed for His purposes. The enemy is viciously apposed to God's purposes in our lives. It is our responsibility to counter the enemy's opposition and overcome him so that we may accomplish God's purpose in our lives.

"Withstand him; be firm in faith (against his onset—rooted, established, strong, immovable, and determined), knowing that the same (identical) sufferings are appointed to your brotherhood (the whole body of Christians) throughout the world." (1 Peter 5:9)

Finally, our goal for overcoming all the opposition and powers of the enemy, is to have freedom to cooperate with, The Holy Spirit, in His work, in conforming us into the image of Jesus Christ. It is to be able to freely praise Jehovah Shalom and to love the brethren. The journey of being conformed into Christlikeness is not a journey without struggles, suffering, and brokenness. Yet, remember Beloved, it is through struggles, sufferings, and brokenness, that we are molded, into our Savior's likeness.

APPENDIX

I have enclosed these verses so that you may see how often God commands His people not to be timid and cowardly (fearful). By inserting the words "timidity and cowardice" where you see the word "fear" you will get a better picture of what God says on this subject.

1. After these things, the word of the Lord came to Abram in a vision, saying, Fear not, Abram, I am your Shield, your abundant compensation, and your reward shall be exceedingly great. (Genesis 15:1)

2. And God heard the voice of the youth, and the angel of God called to Hagar out of heaven and said to her, What troubles you, Hagar? Fear not, for God has heard the voice of the youth where he is. (Genesis 21:17)

3. And the Lord appeared to him the same night and said; I am the God of Abraham your father. Fear not, for I am with you and will favor you with blessings and multiply your descendants for the sake of My servant Abraham. (Genesis 26:24)

4. Moses told the people, Fear not; stand still (firm, confident, undismayed) and see the salvation of the Lord, which

He will work for you today. For the Egyptians you have seen today you shall never see again. (Exodus 14:13)

5. And Moses said to the people, Fear not; for God has come to prove you, so that the (*reverential*) fear of Him may be before you, that you may not sin. (Exodus 20:20)

6. Only do not rebel against the Lord, neither fear the people of the land, for they are bread for us. Their defense and the shadow (*of protection*) is removed from over them, but the Lord is with us. Fear them not. (Numbers 14:9)

7. Behold, the Lord your God has set the land before you; go up and possess it, as the Lord, the God of your fathers, has said to you. Fear not, neither be dismayed. (Deuteronomy 1:21)

8. And the Lord said to me, Do not fear him, for I have given him and all his people and his land into your hand; and you shall do to him as you did to Sihon king of the Amorites, who lived at Heshbon. (Deuteronomy 3:2)

9. You shall not fear them, for the Lord your God shall fight for you. (Deuteronomy 3:22)

10. It is the Lord Who goes before you; He will (march) with you; He will not fail you or let you go or forsake you; (let there be no **cowardice** or flinching, but) fear not, neither become broken (in spirit - depressed, dismayed, and unnerved with alarm). (Deuteronomy 31:8)

11. And shall say to them, Hear, O Israel, you draw near this day to battle against your enemies. Let not your (*minds and*) hearts faint; fear not, and do not tremble or be terrified (*and in dread*) because of them. (Deuteronomy 20:3)

12. Be strong, courageous, and firm; fear not nor be in terror before them, for it is the Lord your God Who goes with you; He will not fail you or forsake you. (Deuteronomy 31:6)

13. It is the Lord Who goes before you; He will (*march*) with you; He will not fail you or let you go or forsake you; (*let there be no cowardice or flinching, but*) fear not, neither become broken (*in spirit—depressed, dismayed, and unnerved with alarm*). (Deuteronomy 31:8)

14. And the Lord said to Joshua, Fear not nor be dismayed. Take all the men of war with you, and arise, go up to Ai; see, I have given into your hand the king of Ai, his people, his city, and his land. (Joshua 8:1)

15. And the Lord said to Joshua, Do not fear them, for I have given them into your hand; there shall not a man of them stand before you. (Joshua 10:8)

16. Joshua said to them, Fear not nor be dismayed; be strong and of good courage. For thus shall the Lord do to all your enemies against whom you fight. (Joshua 10:25)

17. And I said to you, I am the Lord your God; fear not the gods of the Amorites, in whose land you dwell. But you have not obeyed My voice. (Judges 6:10)

18. The Lord said to him, Peace be to you, do not fear; you shall not die. (Judges 6:23)

19. And now, my daughter, fear not. I will do for you all you require, for all my people in the city know that you are a woman of strength (worth, bravery, capability). (Ruth 3:11)

20. And Samuel said to the people, Fear not. You have indeed done all this evil; yet turn not aside from following the Lord, but serve Him with all your heart. (1 Samuel 12:20)

21. Stay with me, fear not; for he who seeks my life seeks your life. But with me you shall be safeguarded. (1 Samuel 22:23)

22. He said to him, Fear not; the hand of Saul my father shall not find you. You shall be king over Israel, and I shall be next to you. Saul my father knows that too. (1 Samuel 23:17)

23. Now Absalom commanded his servants, Notice now, when Amnon's heart is merry with wine and when I say to you, Strike Amnon, then kill him. Fear not; have I not commanded you? Be courageous and brave. (2 Samuel 13:28)

24. (*Elisha*) answered, Fear not; for those with us are more than those with them. (2 Kings 6:16)

25. And the statutes, ordinances, law, and commandment which He wrote for you, you shall observe and do forevermore; you shall not fear other gods. (2 Kings 17:37)

26. And the covenant that I have made with you, you shall not forget; you shall not fear other gods. (2 Kings 17:38)

27. Then you will prosper if you are careful to keep and fulfill the statutes and ordinances with which the Lord charged Moses concerning Israel. Be strong and of good courage. Dread not and fear not; be not dismayed. (1 Chronicles 22:13)

28. Also David told Solomon his son, Be strong and courageous, and do it. Fear not, be not dismayed, for the Lord God, my God, is with you. He will not fail or forsake you until you have finished all the work for the service of the house of the Lord. (1 Chronicles 28:20)

29. You shall not need to fight in this battle; take your positions, stand still, and see the deliverance of the Lord (*Who is*) with you, O Judah and Jerusalem. Fear not nor be dismayed. Tomorrow go out against them, for the Lord is with you. (2 Chronicles 20:17)

30. Because I feared the great multitude and the contempt of families terrified me so that I kept silence and did not go out of the door. Job 31:34

31. Though a host encamp against me, my heart shall not fear; though war arise against me, (*even then*) in this will I be confident. (Psalms 27:3)

32. Therefore we will not fear, though the earth should change and though the mountains be shaken into the midst of the seas, (Psalms 46:2)

33. By (*the help of*) God I will praise His word; on God I lean, rely, and confidently put my trust; I will not fear. What can man, who is flesh, do to me? (Psalms 56:4)

34. The Lord is on my side; I will not fear. What can man do to me? (*Heb. 13:6.*) (Psalms 118:6)

35. And say to him, Take heed and be quiet; fear not, neither be fainthearted because of these two stumps of smoking firebrands—at the fierce anger of (*the Syrian King*) Rezin

and Syria and of the son of Remaliah (*Pekah, usurper of the throne of Israel*). (Isaiah 7:4)

36. Do not call conspiracy (*or hard, or holy*) all that this people will call conspiracy (*or hard, or holy*); neither be in fear of what they fear, nor (*make others afraid and*) in dread. (Isaiah 8:12)

37. Say to those who are of a fearful and hasty heart, Be strong, fear not! Behold, your God will come with vengeance; with the recompense of God He will come and save you. (Isaiah 35:4)

38. Fear not (*there is nothing to fear*), for I am with you; do not look around you in terror and be dismayed, for I am your God. I will strengthen and harden you to difficulties, yes, I will help you; yes, I will hold you up and retain you with My (*victorious*) right hand of rightness and justice. (*Acts 18:10.*) (Isaiah 41:10)

39. For I the Lord your God hold your right hand; I am the Lord, Who says to you, Fear not; I will help you! (Isaiah 41:13)

40. Fear not, you worm Jacob, you men of Israel! I will help you, says the Lord; your Redeemer is the Holy One of Israel. (Isaiah 41:14)

41. But now (*in spite of past judgments for Israel's sins*), thus says the Lord, He Who created you, O Jacob, and He Who formed you, O Israel: Fear not, for I have redeemed you (*ransomed you by paying a price instead of leaving you captives*); I have called you by your name; you are Mine. (Isaiah 43:1)

42. Fear not, for I am with you; I will bring your offspring from the east (*where they are dispersed*) and gather you from the west. (*Acts 18:10.*) (Isaiah 43:5)

43. Thus says the Lord, Who made you and formed you from the womb, Who will help you: Fear not, O Jacob, My servant, and you Jeshurun (*the upright one—applied to Israel as a type of the Messiah*), whom I have chosen. (Isaiah 44:2)

44. Fear not, nor be afraid (*in the coming violent upheavals*); have I not told it to you from of old and declared it? And you are My witnesses! Is there a God besides Me? There is no (*other*) Rock; I know not any. (Isaiah 44:8)

45. Listen to Me, you who know rightness and justice and right standing with God, the people in whose heart is My law and My instruction: fear not the reproach of men, neither be afraid nor dismayed at their reviling. (Isaiah 51:7)

46. Fear not, for you shall not be ashamed; neither be confounded and depressed, for you shall not be put to shame. For you shall forget the shame of your youth, and you shall not (*seriously*) remember the reproach of your widowhood any more. (Isaiah 54:4)

47. You shall establish yourself in righteousness (rightness, in conformity with God's will and order): you shall be far from even the thought of oppression or destruction, for you shall not fear, and from terror, for it shall not come near you. (Isaiah 54:14)

48. Who would not fear You, O King of the nations? For it is fitting to You and Your due! For among all the wise (*men or gods*) of the nations and in all their kingdoms, there is none like You. (Jeremiah 10:7)

49. Therefore fear not, O My servant Jacob, says the Lord, nor be dismayed or cast down, O Israel; for behold, I will save you out of a distant land (*of exile*) and your posterity from the land of their captivity. Jacob will return and will be quiet and at ease, and none will make him afraid or cause him to be terrorized and to tremble. (Jeremiah 30:10)

50. But fear not, O My servant Jacob, and be not dismayed, O Israel. For behold, I will save you from afar, and your offspring from the land of their exile; and Jacob will return and be quiet and at ease, and none will make him afraid. (Jeremiah 46:27)

51. Fear not, O Jacob My servant, says the Lord, for I am with you. For I will make a full and complete end of all the nations to which I have driven you; yet I will not make a full end of you. But I will chasten and correct you in just measure, and I will not hold you guiltless by any means or leave you unpunished. (Jeremiah 46:28)

52. Like an adamant harder than flint or a diamond point have I made your forehead; fear them not, neither be dismayed at their looks, for they are a rebellious house. (*Isa. 50:7; Jer. 1:18; 15:20; Mic. 3:8.*) (Ezekiel 3:9)

53. Then he said to me, Fear not, Daniel, for from the first day that you set your mind and heart to understand and to humble yourself before your God, your words were heard, and I have come as a consequence of (*and in response to*) your words. (Daniel 10:12)

54. And he said, O man greatly beloved, fear not! Peace be to you! Be strong, yes, be strong. And when he had spoken to me, I was strengthened and said, Let my lord speak, for you have strengthened me. (Daniel 10:19)

55. Fear not, O land; be glad and rejoice, for the Lord has done great things! (*Zech. 12:8-10.*) (Joel 2:21)

56. According to the promise that I covenanted with you when you came out of Egypt, so My Spirit stands and abides in the midst of you; fear not. (Haggai 2:5)

57. And as you have been a curse and a byword among the nations, O house of Judah and house of Israel, so will I save you, and you shall be a blessing. Fear not, but let your hands be strong and hardened. (*Jer. 22:8, 9.*) (Zechariah 8:13)

58. So again have I purposed in these days to do good to Jerusalem and to the house of Judah. Fear not! (Zechariah 8:15)

59. But Jesus, on hearing this, answered him, Do not be seized with alarm or struck with fear; simply believe (*in Me as able to do this*), and she shall be made well. (Luke 8:50)

60. But (*even*) the very hairs of your head are all numbered. Do not be struck with fear or seized with alarm; you are of greater worth than many (*flocks*) of sparrows. (Luke 12:7)

61. Do not be seized with alarm and struck with fear, little flock, for it is your Father's good pleasure to give you the kingdom! (Luke 12:32)

62. And He said to them, Go and tell that fox (sly and crafty, skulking and **coward**ly), Behold, I drive out demons and perform healings today and tomorrow, and on the third day I finish (complete) My course. (Luke 13:32)

63. ALSO (Jesus) told them a parable to the effect that they ought always to pray and not to turn **coward** (faint, lose heart, and give up). (Luke 18:1)

64. Do not fear, O Daughter of Zion! Look! Your King is coming, sitting on a donkey's colt! (*Zech. 9:9.*) (John 12:15)

65. And yet (*in spite of all this*) many even of the leading men (the authorities and the nobles) believed and trusted in Him. But because of the Pharisees they did not confess it, for fear that (*if they should acknowledge Him*) they would be expelled from the synagogue; (John 12:42)

66. Peace I leave you; My (own) peace I now give and bequeath to you. **Not** as the world gives do I give to you. Do **not** let your heart be troubled, neither let them be afraid. (Stop allowing yourselves to be agitated and disturbed; and do **not** permit yourselves to be fearful and intimidated and cowardly and unsettled.) (John 14:27)

67. And one night the Lord said to Paul in a vision, Have no fear, but speak and do not keep silent; (Acts 18:9)

68. For (*the Spirit which*) you have now received (*is*) not a spirit of slavery to put you once more in bondage to fear, but you have received the Spirit of adoption (*the Spirit producing sonship*) in (*the bliss of*) which we cry, Abba (Father)! Father! Romans 8:15)

69. Therefore we do not become discouraged (utterly spirit-less, exhausted, and wearied out through fear). Though our outer man is (*progressively*) decaying and wasting away, yet our inner self is being (*progressively*) renewed day after day. Corinthians 4:16)

70. So I ask you not to lose heart (*not to faint or become despondent through fear*) at what I am suffering in your behalf. (*Rather glory in it*) for it is an honor to you. (Ephesians 3:13)

71. For God did not give us a spirit of timidity (of cowardice, of craven and cringing and fawning fear), but (*He has given us a spirit*) of power and of love and of calm and well-balanced mind and discipline and self-control. (2 Timothy 1:7)

72. So we take comfort and are encouraged and confidently and boldly say, The Lord is my Helper; I will not be seized with alarm (*I will not fear or dread or be terrified*). What can man do to me? (*Ps. 27:1;118:6.*) (Hebrews 13:6)

73. There is no fear in love (*dread does not exist*), but full-grown (complete, perfect) love turns fear out of doors and expels every trace of terror! For fear brings with it the thought of punishment
and (*so*) he who is afraid has not reached the full maturity of love (*is not yet grown into love's complete perfection*). (1 John 4:18)

74. Fear nothing that you are about to suffer. (Dismiss your dread and your fears!) Behold, the devil is indeed about to throw some of you into prison, that you may be tested and proved and critically appraised, and for ten days you will have affliction. Be loyally faithful unto death (even if you must die for it), and I will give you the crown of life. (Revelation 2:10)

ADDITIONAL INFORMATION REFERENCE

❧

Apostolic Tradition:

* Early Christian History,
http://www.sirreadalot.org/christianity/christianity/early-christianhistoryR.htm.

* Christian Attitudes and Activities: worship, The Sacraments & Education:
From AD 70 to AD 363, by Harlie Kay Gallatin
http://www.sbuniv.edu/~hgallatin/ht3663le09.html

* The Apostolic Tradition of Hippolytus of Rome:
http://www.bombax.com/hippolytus.htm.

GOD'S DISQUALIFING LIST

❧

"But as for the cowards and the ignoble and the contemptible and the cravenly lacking in courage and the cowardly submissive, and as for the unbelieving and faithless, and as for the depraved and defiled with abominations, and as for murderers and the lewd and adulterous and the practicers of magic arts and the idolaters (those who give supreme devotion to anyone or anything other than God) and all liars (those who knowingly convey untruth by word or deed)—(all of these shall have) their part in the lake that blazes with fire and brimstone. This is the second death." (Revelation 21:8)

- The Cowards
- The Ignoble
- The Contemptible
- The Cravenly lacking in courage
- The Cowardly submissive
- The Unbelieving
- The Faithless
- The Deprave
- The Defiled with abominations
- The Lewd
- The Adulterous
- The Practitioner's of magic arts

- The Idolaters (Those who give supreme devotion to anyone or anything other than God)
- The Lairs (Those who knowingly convey untruth by word or deed)

SOLDIER'S CREED

"He who dwells in the secret place, of the Most High, shall remain stable and fixed under the shadow of the Almighty (Whose power, no foe can withstand). I will say of the Lord, He is my Refuge and my Fortress, my God; on Him, I lean and rely, and in Him, I (confidently) trust! For (then) He will deliver you from the snare of the fowler and from the deadly pestilence. (Then) He will cover you with His pinions, and under His wings shall you trust and find refuge; His truth and His faithfulness are a shield and a buckler. You shall not be afraid of the terror of the night, nor of the arrow (the evil plots and slanders of the wicked) that flies by day, Nor of the pestilence that stalks in darkness, nor of the destruction and sudden death that surprise and lay waste at noonday. A thousand may fall at your side, and ten thousand at your right hand, but it shall not come near you. Only a spectator shall you be (yourself inaccessible in the secret place of the Most High) as you witness the reward of the wicked. Because you have made the Lord your refuge, and the Most High your dwelling place, (Ps. 91:1, 14.) There shall no evil befall you, nor any plague or calamity come near your tent. For He, will give His angels (especial) charge over you, to accompany and defend and preserve you in all your ways (of obedience and service). They shall bear you up on their hands,

lest you dash your foot against a stone. (Luke 4:10, 11; Heb. 1:14.) You shall tread upon the lion and adder; the young lion and the serpent shall you trample underfoot. (Luke 10:19.) Because he has set his love upon Me, therefore will I deliver him; I will set him on high, because he knows and understands My name (has a personal knowledge of My mercy, love, and kindness—trusts and relies on Me, knowing I will never forsake him, no, never). He shall call upon Me, and I will answer him; I will be with him in trouble, I will deliver him and honor him. With long life will I satisfy him and show him My salvation."
(Psalm 91 entire chapter)

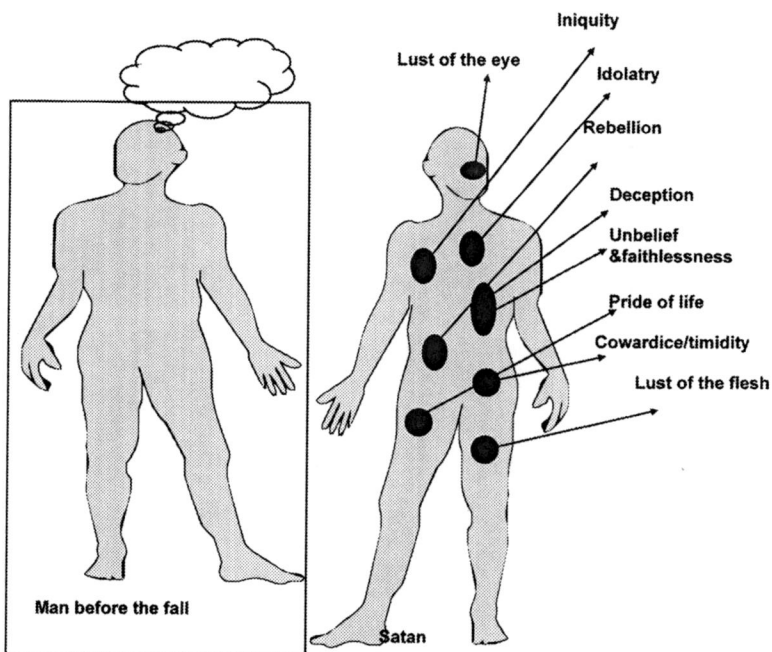

Man before the fall

Iniquity

Lust of the eye

Idolatry

Rebellion

Deception

Unbelief &faithlessness

Pride of life

Cowardice/timidity

Lust of the flesh

Satan

ABOUT THE AUTHOR

⮜⮞

Joyce Toney and her husband, Guenther founded Application Word Ministries in Germany and Joyce is the founder of Application Word Ministries in Ghana. She has served God's people as Bible teacher and Pastor for over 22 years. Through the help of her co-laborers in Ghana she has helped establish five churches in Ghana.

Joyce has taught sound doctrine from the Bible, trained believers, and brought deliverance, to countless souls bound by the enemy of their souls. God has used her to bring healing to others as a result of living in a fallen world.

Joyce is the author of "The Noahide Laws: Humanity's Obligation to God", a book that now brings deliverance to both Christians and non-Christians.

Her depth of biblical knowledge is derived from her diligent study of the Word of God, as well as the mighty teaching of the Holy Spirit. Her desire is to see God's people live in the freedom of His Word and to walk worthy of the call which God has called all the saints of His Body in Christ Jesus.

Printed in the United States
80095LV00002B/1-75